What people are s

Folktales, Faeries, and Spirits

Practical, hands on and wonderfully magical, this inclusive and accessible guide to navigating the faery realm is creative, original and utterly delightful.

Anna McKerrow, author of *The Bird Atlas*, *The Book of Babalon* and the *Greenworld Trilogy*

This book will be of particular interest to students of Druidry interested in working with folklore, landscape and spirits of place. There are many interesting fairy insights here, and the author provides a valuable map for engaging with stories and spirits in your landscape.

Nimue Brown, author of *Druidry and the Ancestors: Finding our place in our own history*, and *Pagan Dreaming: The Magic of Altered Consciousness*

In *Folktales, Faeries, and Spirits* you will find practical ways for working with faeries and spirits, integrating those practices into your everyday life, and also approaching folklore as the living, breathing, moving body of work that it still is - not something static, or confined to dusty books and old wives' tales. Quin invites you to thoroughly examine your own beliefs and magical actions with useful questions in each chapter, and encourages a practice that finds us, quite literally, where we are.

Kate Garrett, author of *To Feed My Woodland Bones [A Changeling's Tale]* and Magical Editor of Mookychick magazine

Halo Quin's *Folktales, Faeries, and Spirits* brings Faery lore to life, retrieving it from the archives and oral traditions, from beneath toadstools and mossy tree stumps. This book is an invitation to open one's eyes to the awareness that we share our homes and landscapes, the Middle Realm, with innumerable Fae Beings, many of whom go unnoticed. For those seeking to correct this oversight and to respectfully (and sensibly!) greet their Fae neighbours, this is a portal to the land of the Fae, which is closer than one might think!

Olivia Church, author of *Isis - Great of Magic, She of 10,000 Names* and *Sekhmet - Lady of Flame, Eye of Ra*

Pagan Portals
Folktales, Faeries, and Spirits

Faery magic from story to practice

Pagan Portals

Folktales, Faeries, and Spirits

Faery magic from story to practice

Halo Quin

MOON
BOOKS

Winchester, UK
Washington, USA

JOHN HUNT PUBLISHING

First published by Moon Books, 2022
Moon Books is an imprint of John Hunt Publishing Ltd., No. 3 East Street, Alresford
Hampshire SO24 9EE, UK
office@jhpbooks.net
www.johnhuntpublishing.com
www.moon-books.net

For distributor details and how to order please visit the 'Ordering' section on our website.

Text copyright: Halo Quin 2021

ISBN: 978 1 78535 941 5
978 1 78535 942 2 (ebook)
Library of Congress Control Number: 2021944451

A CIP catalogue record for this book is available from the British Library.

Design: Matthew Greenfield

UK: Printed and bound by CPI Group (UK) Ltd, Croydon, CR0 4YY
Printed in North America by CPI GPS partners

We operate a distinctive and ethical publishing philosophy in
all areas of our business, from our global network of authors to
production and worldwide distribution.

Contents

Previous Titles

Your Faery Heart
B00932SH6U

Pixie Kisses
978-1447523444

Pagan Portals – Your Faery Magic
978-1785350764

Pagan Portals – Gods and Goddesses of Wales
978-1785356216

Twisted – Honest Reflections of a Kinky Witch
978-1916339644

*All That Glitters – Wonderings & Wanderings
of a Changeling Bard*
978-1916339651

For mum, who introduced me to the spirits of the land.
For my brothers, who joined in with my earliest storytelling adventures.
And for all you bards and storytellers, carrying the keys to magic in your hearts.

Preface

A Note from the Author

Faeries, as with most spirits, are varied and shifting. The term can cover so many different types of beings, and many different forms of magic… even within one culture. In the Neopagan community (that wonderful, multifaceted melting pot of magic, polytheism, and earth-loving) you may encounter a couple of dichotomies when the subject of faeries arises.

There are those who love the fair folk and call on them at every opportunity, and those that may grudgingly acknowledge them, but no more, for fear of mischief. You, too, are likely to encounter folk who adore all that is faery, considering them to be spirits of pure goodness, and those who warn you that they are dangerous, or at least prone to stealing shiny things, and must be avoided. The truth is somewhat more nuanced, and your relationship with these spirits will depend on many things, not least whether or not they take a shine to you. Think of them as very distinctly real people, with their own desires, motivations, and personalities, and you won't go far wrong. Some fae are kind, some cruel, and some certainly seem to enjoy causing trouble. Who you meet will shape your experiences as much as how you behave. As one who has always heard their call, I hope that what I share helps others on the same journey to connect with those that like to help us out, and to spot the more dangerous areas of the wildwood before they stumble into somewhere they have not been invited… yet.

Another debate among humans who talk about faeries is whether they are nature spirits and spirits of the land, or simply an otherworldly race of humanoids. There are historical threads suggesting that both might be true. And again, the lines between the two are far less solid than we'd like to think… The simplest

1

way to reconcile the conflicts is to recognise that "faery" is a broad term which has been applied to many different spirits, and how wide your definition is will be influenced by your cultural background, experience, and encounters. Throughout this book I will remind you that the fae that live in your landscape may be different to those that I know, and that the key to this work is in building your own relationship with them and working out your own edges in practice, rather than just in theory.

For me, there is a feel to faery beings which distinguishes them from, say, angels, gods, elementals, animal spirits, or other types of spirits, but your experience may vary. Within this text I've gone back to the stories and drawn on my experiences and research to offer some more or less concrete connections, but, just like the fair folk themselves, you may well find the boundaries and definitions shifting for you over time.

In all that we do in this work, however, relationship is central. Whether you are seeking to understand the fae to avoid causing trouble, or you hear their call and wish to find some tips for navigating this path without making some of the more obvious mistakes, there are clues to building a good relationship with our otherworldly cousins, as wonderful and temperamental as they may or may not be. Much like us, really.

This work is very important to me, and in offering it to you I am trusting you to adapt and amend it to your practice, and the spirits you encounter along the path, with respect for those that dance on the edges of our everyday senses.

Welcome (back) to the bonny road to fair Elfland, my dear.

~Halo x

Introduction

Preparing for an Adventure

Some Important Concepts

As this book is designed to be a practical guide, rather than having a lot of theory at the beginning I've woven it through each chapter, but if this is the first time you've picked up a book like this you may find some of the concepts benefit from a little clarification... And if this isn't your first encounter with them then it might help to know how I use these terms.

Firstly, "spirits". I use this in a broad sense, to refer to the non embodied beings. Faeries, then – like gods, ghosts, and angels – are a type of spirit. I prefer to distinguish between literary and pop culture fiction "fairies" and the spirits and beings found in folklore and witchcraft with a slightly less common spelling, "faeries". This is a personal choice, so don't worry if you see them used differently elsewhere.

Folklore includes the practices and beliefs woven into a culture at an everyday and "everyman" type level, such as that found within so-called superstition, folk and fairy tales, and the oral tradition.

And magic, well... put simply magic is the art and practice of changing the world, or at least part of it, through energetic and spiritual means.

Getting Started

The only tools which I would suggest are essential for the work in this book are a journal of some kind and a writing implement. I recommend writing by hand on paper if you can as it allows your mind to process things differently to typing, and gives you a physical record of what you discover as you go. Technology can also find spirit contact and energies disruptive, though not always, so paper and pen is more reliable for this kind of work. If handwriting isn't possible then do, please use the technology that works for you. Dictation, drawing, and music making are all methods that you may choose to use.

I also suggest that throughout this book you practice trusting your intuition. If anything feels wrong for you, don't do it at that time. Perhaps explore in your journal why it feels wrong, perhaps your spirit guides are guiding you to focus somewhere else, or perhaps you're resisting something that would help you heal something you're not ready to heal. There are many reasons, all of them valid. Trust your instincts, and if this is something you have trouble doing, now is a good time to start practicing. It'll get easier over time.

On a similar note, please feel free to adapt any of the exercises to your own abilities and situations. Not everyone can get outside. Not everyone can light candles in their home. We each process sensory information differently – some of us see psychically, others hear, some of us cannot connect with one sense at all, on a physical or psychic level. We all have our own strengths. You are in charge of your own experience. Trust yourself to do what you need to do with the information and exercises within.

How to Use This Book

This book is written as a practical guidebook, one which will take you step by step through the stages of engaging with folk and faery stories (and myths and legends, for that matter) to tease out the threads of faery magic; the what, the why, the how, and the when. Each chapter is loosely themed around an aspect of this practice, but they do build on each other.

This means the best way to use this book on first reading is to work through the material from beginning to end, allowing the practical exercises to build on each other. If you are new to magical practice, this will give you a strong foundation and understanding of what is involved, as well as the support to engage with working with the fae sensibly.

Each chapter has discussions of theory, thoughts to consider when building your practice and taking steps to initiate or deepen your relationship with spirit beings, as well as practical exercises to develop your magical craft. At the end of each chapter are suggestions for integrating what you've done in that chapter into the previous work, and questions to consider, which may help you deepen your understanding further.

I recommend taking your time with each chapter, and keeping a journal of your adventures. This will help you to see how your magic has developed and bring the numinous, otherworldly experiences more into the everyday realm for you.

You may, of course, choose to jump into later chapters that appeal to you, and explore the theory in whichever order you choose, but for your first time engaging with the practical aspects, please exercise discernment as many of them build on the previous material and are safest (and easiest) when performed in the order I've shared them.

As I have noted in previous books, even though some readers have expressed discomfort with the idea; I do absolutely encourage you to write in your copy of this book (even if only in the margins, and even if only in pencil) and annotate the material here. Let your engagement with this magic be a two way conversation. Let your experiences and understanding of it shape how you view that which I share with you. And as your understanding evolves and deepens over time, you'll find your earlier self reminding your later self of wonderful clues you've already found, and your later self can write back to you now, with the wisdom, beauty, and joy gathered along the way. As a compromise, if marking up the pages is too uncomfortable, then perhaps consider using sticky notes to hold your conversation with the material... and maybe, if I may be a little provocative in my framing, contemplate why it is that what *I've* written in this book might hold more weight to you than your own thoughts on the matter?

Chapter 1

Under the Hawthorn Tree

What is Folkloric Faery Magic?

Faery magic is working magic in relationship with faery spirits, who I describe primarily as spirits with close ties to the land and the "green" world. I've spent my entire life working with the Fae in one way or another, from greeting them everywhere as a child, to my current practice of prayer, honouring the Land Spirits, storytelling to share their magic, and journeying to Faeryland (in a manner often described in modern pagan circles as "shamanic").

Alongside my practical work, I have studied them through folklore and folktales, and investigated other theories of spirits and spirit contact. The theoretical roots of this book in folklore and story is why I describe this as "Folkloric". The tales contain keys for understanding ways of approaching them that have worked in the past, and clues for pitfalls to avoid! Between the research and my practice, I have developed what I playfully call my "faeosophy", or faery philosophy.

There is a relatively modern way of working with the Fae that works with a particular form of fairies, based in a merging of the literary ideas of fairies from Victorian South-East England – the descendants of the beings found in folktales who are often small and much like the famous flower fairies of Cicely Mary Barker, a lineage described beautifully by Diane Purkiss – with the elementals of Paracelsus from the 16th century, i.e. beings which embody the four magical "elements" of earth, air, fire and water, known as gnomes, sylphs, salamanders, and undines respectively, found in alchemical and ceremonial texts. This is what many people think of when they hear the words "fairy magic", and it is a valid way of working with that particular kind of being, but this blend seems to be a relatively recent model of working with roots in theosophy, which encourages a view of faeries as diminutive. In the folkloric traditions they may be small, or linked to specific elements, but are often powerful beings of the same or greater status as ourselves, and definitely greater power. This "New Age" model, exemplified in Doreen Virtue's work, is a very popular, and very safe, way of approaching spirit beings as it focuses on a specific set of spirits. If, however, you find yourself drawn to, curious about, or indeed encountering, Fae spirits outside of this group then the folkloric path may hold the keys you need! In my book *Pagan Portals – Your Faery Magic*, I've shared a blend of folkloric threads and New Age/modern pagan tools to introduce individuals to the building of an effective magical relationship with faeries and your inner connection to that thread of magic. In this book, however, I've kept to what we can find in the tales and applied it using practical methods of building a working relationship with the spirits.

Being from Northern Europe my work has focused on the lore and magic of these lands. As a result, this book focuses on stories and specifics from the areas which I am familiar with. If you live in a different land, however, then it is important for you to apply the principles to your own folklore. I strongly recommend that you find stories from your locale, specific to the place in which you live, to learn more. Here in the wilds of Wales I learn from Y Mabinogi and Welsh faery tales, but when I travel to Edinburgh it is the tales of the city and selkies of the Scottish Sea that I look to, and in Spain the stories and spirits are different again. Personally, I also work a lot with the Nordic fae because they have found me wherever I've been; being great travellers there are few places the Alfar haven't touched. The faery cultures vary with the landscape, the trees which they are connected to, their names, the best offerings to give them. All of these details will be found in your local tales.

There can also be other spirits present, who have their own traditions, and it may not be appropriate for you to approach them without the guidance of someone from that tradition. For example, the spirits who look after indigenous Australian cultures may not take kindly to a Brit like myself wading in, calling them elves and pouring them a cup of cream. (Though, on the other hand, some of them may enjoy this, I haven't had the opportunity to ask them!) It is very much like the way we have different human cultures and ways of being polite. The spirits in different places have different ways of interacting with the humans that live there, and the stories of the place act as guidebooks to these relations. The same goes for finding local trees and features of the landscape. For example, in Ireland the faeries often live in specific trees, but in Iceland you hear of rocks being their homes, and in Wales you will certainly find a Goblin Stone or two.

As a question to begin with, then: Where would you look in your landscape for the fae?

Under The Hawthorn Tree

TRUE THOMAS lay on grassy bank,
And he beheld a lady gay,
A lady that was brisk and bold,
Come riding over the fernie brae.

Her skirt was of the grass-green silk,
Her mantel of the velvet fine,
And on every lock of her horse's mane
Hung fifty silver bells and nine.

The tale of True Thomas, or *Thomas the Rhymer*, is an old one from the wild borderlands of Scotland (in the North of the UK), though working with faeries and otherworldly spirits is certainly older. The earliest recorded version of Thomas' story is recorded in a manuscript dating from around 1430-1440, and Thomas of Erceldoune, of whom the tale is written, lived two hundred years before that. The ballad which his story is most often told through nowadays was recorded in the early 1800s, and it keeps many of the key images from the earlier manuscript, demonstrating the strength of those images and their value as signposts to encounters with the fae. A version of the ballad can be found in the appendices with the language anglicised and modernised for my readers.

Thomas the Rhymer is the story of how a bard gained the gift of prophecy from the Fair Folk, and it begins on the bank of a river, under a tree (most often seen as a hawthorn), where the Queen of Elfland comes across a sleeping Thomas. She invites him to come away to her land, and they travel across vast rivers and past apple trees. He is taken into her service for seven years and warned to not speak a word whilst he is in Faeryland. At the end of his service to the Queen she gives him the gift of the tongue which cannot lie.

In these images we can find doorways to magical states and magical lands, guidance for developing a relationship with the fae folk and a structure through which we can build our own practices.

What are Faeries? Clues from the Queen

In all my time working with the fae I've come across many explanations for what they might be or how they may have come into being.

The description of the Queen in *Thomas the Rhymer* as a beautiful lady in green silk, on a fine horse with bells in its mane gives us a few clues as to the nature of faeries. The green colour shows her role as part of the green world and the land, her horse shows her power and the bells ring with the music of Faeryland. Beauty and music are signs of the way in which faery magic enchants us and conjures a sense of wonder – which encourages an openness to the world. It also reminds us that they are quite capable of showing us what we want to see in order to gain our trust. The specific location and Thomas historical status illustrate that the Fae are often connected to specific, real, places, the river and the hawthorn tree are also notable as water is often a gateway to Faeryland and the hawthorn is said to guard the entrance with its thorns, whilst the beauty of its blossoms open us to the sense of wonder required for travel between the worlds.

From both my experiences and the stories in which they feature I have come to the conclusion that the fae not simply one kind of being, but are a collection of related beings and powers, or spirits and energies, who embody the untamed magic of the land and the natural world. They can be guardians of places, they are most often part of the green world or the water or stones, and they are very closely related to spirits of the dead. As spirits without bodies, they are shapeshifters and so appear differently at different times, they are not limited as we are but they have a definite consciousness. They appear to me to be connected to the earth and the land, much as we are. They make choices, have names and hold their own ethics and rules which differ from ours. I will touch on all these points as we progress through the chapters and give indications of why I hold each of these beliefs, but for now I thought it worth clarifying what I mean when I say Faery; In short, they are the other-than-human spirits who inhabit the same spirit realms that we do, even to the extent of taking physical form for their own ends at times, as they reside close to the planes that we ourselves do.

In *Wights and Ancestors*, scholar and practitioner Jenny Blain lists faeries as a sub-category of spirit - separate from land-spirits and elves, among others – but also notes that in practice it is very common for those lines to be permeable and the classifications themselves to blur. This fits with my experience, and with the way in which the folktales themselves sometimes use the terms interchangeably. Just as one would distinguish between the alder and blackthorn when working with trees, so too we can (and should) distinguish in our practice between, for example, brownies, elves, land spirits, and faery ladies. But when we engage in this method of discovering and building our relationship with those that we meet, we can apply the same principles as our starting point for this work. I will tend to use faery as a catch-all term, and leave it to you to recall the vast variety of Folk sheltered under that umbrella.

Practice 1. Altars and Shrines

Traditionally, offerings to the fae who share our homes would be made by the hearth, or outside the door, to encourage good feelings between them and us. Cotton ribbons and strips of cloth from natural fabrics may be tied to certain trees as wishes or blessings, and drinks would be poured as libations at the base of trees. These practices are still seen today in the ribbons on "cloutie" trees by sacred wells, and cider poured over the roots of apple trees in wassailing. In many cultures throughout history, one would find household shrines to various gods – Hecate would have a shrine in the entrance to many houses in ancient Greece, just as Ganesh does in many Hindu homes. Heathen homes throughout Germanic tribe lands would have Hoffs dedicated to their gods, or cairns outside for the dead or the land wights. There is a long history of locations dedicated to spirit beings, and the fae are no different. In folklore there are often specific trees or rocks which are home to the local fae, and in Practice 2 we will go looking for some of these, but for now we'll use the more formal structure of an altar or shrine.

If we wish to honour something or to invite it into our lives then we need to make space for it. An altar can be such a place, and can act as a reminder each day that this is something we are choosing to work with. If you already have an altar you might like to make another one specifically for this work, or a space on your main altar dedicated to your faery work.

Find a space in your home where you can keep a few objects. A flat surface such as a shelf or the top of a bookcase can work well, or you can use a small box if leaving items out is not an option, opening the box and engaging with the items for a period each day. This can be good in a household with small children, cats, or unsympathetic housemates around for example!

Think about the images in the *Ballad of Thomas the Rhymer*. Perhaps you can find a picture or small statue of a lady in green, or a white horse, or a small tree. A candle is useful and very atmospheric, and a nice, small bowl of water which you can refill is a good representation of the river, and water in general which can act as a gateway to Faeryland. You might choose to include something that represents faeries more generally, or the land on which you live. Spend a bit of time this week gathering items and creating a space in which to house them. Once you have your altar you can use it for reflecting on the work you are doing, as a space for making magical things, or simply a shrine to enchantment to encourage it in your life.

Consider the way this might work best for you right now, and begin there. Remember, this is an entirely personal space and can be added to and changed over time, as feels right for you.

Practice 2. A Faery Wander

If you can this week, spend some time wandering outside, soaking up the feeling of being out in nature (or as much nature as you can safely reach). Begin to notice places in your neighbourhood that might be magical, good for meeting faeries, or quiet enough for some meditation. See if you recognise any trees or plants. Note down anything you notice which might be important, or which makes you smile.

Don't be fooled by the seeming simplicity of this practice; taking time to be really mindful of the landscape around you is good practice for engaging in connecting with the world. This is the beginning of opening yourself to an awareness of the otherworld which lies intertwined with the manifest realm, and opening your eyes to Seeing faery spirits and getting to know your local area.

Practice 3. The Hawthorn Tree

The hawthorn tree is well-known for being a faery tree. It is often found in British hedgerows but when it stands alone it is a meeting place for the fae. Its leaves and berries are edible (though be careful when eating wild berries!) and its flowers are associated with May Day, when the land bursts into blossom each year. Its abundance of offerings to travellers has earned hawthorn the colloquial title of the "bread and cheese tree" in certain places. The combination of beauty and thorns tells you that this tree contains the magic of opposites, and it protects the beauty and magic of faery for the traveller between the worlds.

Hawthorn (*Crataegus monogyna*)

Once you know how to spot this tree, you'll see it everywhere in Britain. It is often small and shrubby with narrow thorns shaped like needles, and small, many lobed leaves. In late spring it blossoms with white foamy bunches of five-petaled blossom, and in the autumn, these become deep red haws. While hawthorn rarely grows large it can reach out wide and will happily create a natural barrier when planted with other hawthorn trees. It protects many small creatures with its thorns. The wood is hard, and even harder when cultivated in a hedgerow, so is good for small carvings such as combs (and vampire stakes!) and burns hot in a fire.

In herbalism Hawthorn is a powerful heart medicine, and magically it opens the heart too. Hawthorn is a gateway tree, protecting and guiding travellers. As a tree of the hedgerow, it is associated with boundaries so one hawthorn alone in a field is unusual, a boundary with nothing to bound, and as such

14

could be a gateway to the otherworld. The blossom signals the start of summer season, Beltane, and May Day festivities, and the warm period where people can get outside and enjoy themselves away from the prying eyes of family... leading to a strong connection with sex and sexuality (which suggests the magic of creativity and sensuality, as well as a "gateway into life" kind of aspect to the tree). It was recommended not to bring hawthorn blossom into the house for fear of bringing in bad luck, though they would be used to crown the May Queen each year.

Research the magic of the hawthorn. If hawthorn trees are not native, or common, where you live, look into the folklore of your area to see which trees are beloved of the spirits of your land. Try to find one near your home, and visit it. See how it feels to sit beneath its branches and read the ballad of *Thomas the Rhymer*. If it feels right, ask the tree if you may leave it a gift of milk (or another drink) in return for one of its twigs, a leaf or two or a flower to place on your altar. If visiting a hawthorn tree is impossible, or there simply aren't any where you live, then find a picture of one to keep on your altar instead and spend a bit of time each day pondering the nature of a tree that opens the way to another world. If you can get to a tree at least once to ask it if you may take a small twig (or a photo) to connect with it at your altar then that is a good thing to do. This way if you can't visit it physically you can spend time with it at your altar. If you absolutely cannot do this yourself, then perhaps someone you trust can go for you. Make sure they are willing to tell the tree that is what it is for and ask if this is ok. This way the tree can work to make a connection with you as well, or tell you to find another, more willing tree-friend if it doesn't want to work in this way.

Once you've done a little bit of research, spend some time contemplating what the nature of the hawthorn tree tells you about the nature of the fair folk.

Practice 4. Your Understanding

This work is about *your* practice, which must be based in your relationship with the fae, and your understanding of their nature which will grow and develop the more you research and interact with them. Take some time to journal about your experiences so far. You might want to consider these questions:

What do you think of when you think of faeries?
What is your experience of faeries or faery/fairy magic?
Does everything you've read so far on the nature of faery beings feel right to you? If not, which bits feel wrong and why?
What does respect mean to you?
What folklore and folktales about your locale do you know already?
What, if anything, has surprised you in your research so far?
Why did you pick up this book? Why are you interested in folkloric faery magic?

You may wish to keep an eye on your dreams during this work, if anything in your dreams strikes you as important or relevant to the fae, make a note of it in your journal.

Starting your Story Exploration

There are some wonderful books full of folklore out there and your local library is a very good place to start for books that explore your area. Generally, if you look for tales about faeries, you'll find Irish, or more generally Western European stories, which are useful starting places even if you don't live in Western Europe for learning to recognise the kinds of beings that fit in this category, even though the lore varies from area to area, sometimes quite dramatically. It is very important to explore more local stories and customs as well though, so don't stop with the typical collections! You will notice that not all "Fairy tales" are about faeries, and so there is a move toward calling them "wonder tales" instead, but even so most of them give clues for interacting with the otherworld or magical situations, beings, and objects.

Here are some good starting points for your reading:

- The website Sacred Texts has a huge amount of Fairy tales, including English Fairy tales, and a whole selection of Celtic Fairy tales.
- The Grimms' Fairy Tales is a major classic collected in Germany by the two brothers, Jakob and Wilhelm Grimm. While you can read them online, such as at Sacred Texts, there is now a beautiful collection of them by a Grimm scholar who has translated them back as close to the original stories that the Grimms recorded as possible. After the brothers first published them, they came under some pressure to edit them for the children of the time, so some of the rougher aspects got polished out of many of the tales. If you can, I recommend *The Original Folk and Fairy Tales of the Brothers Grimm*, translated and edited by Jack Zipes.
- In Britain there are marvellous collections of folklore based in each county, published by The History Press, including *Ceredigion Folk Tales* by Peter Stevenson, and others in that range, or covering a broader area such as *Dancing with Trees – Eco-Tales from the British Isles* by Allison Galbraith and Alette J Willis.

Check out the resources section at the end of this book, and investigate the local history and folklore sections in your library and nearby museums. You may even find local folklore enthusiasts and storytelling circles to join, which can be wonderful source of living lore. Have a dig around the forest of wonder, allow yourself to be led off the path by lights in the distance and see where your journey takes you.

Questions to Ponder

It can be useful to reflect on information we learn and put it into our own words, and to explore our own journey, so each chapter I'll include some questions for you to ponder and write about if you choose.

What are faeries?

Why is Thomas the Rhymer a good story to work with?

What is the foundation of a good relationship with the Fair Folk?

What is a faery altar for?

Why do you want to engage in this work?

What might be some of the ways you can approach them respectfully and with caution?

What is your experience of the Fair Folk so far?

Chapter 2

Opening the Way

True Thomas he took off his hat,
And bowed down to his knee:
"All hail, mighty Queen of Heaven!
For your peer on earth I never did see."

"O no, O no, True Thomas," she says,
"That name does not belong to me;
I am but the queen of fair Elfland,
And I've come here to visit thee."

In Chapter 1 we covered some of the background for working with folkloric faery magic and signalled to both our deepest selves and the faery realm that we wish to work with these spirits. We began to explore the landscape and the stories in which we will find the faery folk as well as the nature of these beings. It's important to be clear on who we are requesting to work with and what their nature is, for example; he Queen of Elfland (Faeryland) is not the "Queen of Heaven" (the Virgin Mary), and faeries are not angelic spirits, though they can share qualities with them. Elfland or Faeryland is often depicted as being within the land, it is not up in the heavenly sky, so faery beings can be recognised as having their *being* in a similar place to us. In many cultures you have three realms, described in Core Shamanism (see Resources) as the upper, lower and middle world. Generally speaking, the gods and angels come from the upper world, the realm of the dead, giants, and primal powers form the lower world. Like us, faeries seem to come from the middle world. In that case, as they are such near cousins, why would we not work with them?

Why Work With the Fae? Some Faeosophy.

We modern, Western, humans often live our lives disconnected from our bodies and from the land. The fae folk are deeply embedded in the land and the living landscape and developing a relationship with them involves coming into a good relationship with the land on which we live and with nature as a whole. Simultaneously we realise that we are part of the natural world and we come back into better relationship with our own bodies and untamed selves.

In terms of working magically with the fae, we also have records of people:

Looking for faeries
Gaining healing powers from them
Seeking treasure
Honouring their places
Atempting to summon Faery Queens for power, support or wish granting
Warding against their ill-will
Leaving offerings in gratitude for support
… and more…

All of this shows that the fae have power and can help us in very practical ways, or can hinder us if we do not have a good relationship with them. This is mirrored in materialistic terms when we look at how a disrespectful attitude towards nature in general has led to a great deal of pollution and ill-health, and even the loss of resources... i.e. wealth!

Basically, a good relationship with the Fair Folk is a good relationship with the land that looks after us, and they can support us in our magical work if we look after them in return, just as the land supports us in our general lives if we treat it with respect. This, in turn, helps to heal us, them and the world around us.

Not all of them want to work with us, even of those that are generally of friendly natures. There are numerous stories where one sibling is kind and generous and is given gifts from the faeries they meet, and another is rude to the same beings and comes away much the worse for it. And there are tales of dangerous otherworldly beings, such as the kelpies who steal young people away to drown them for their dinner. In the New Age model, fairies are generally beings of light and always willing to grant wishes in return for offerings. In the folkloric traditions some of the fae are powerful allies, but that same power means that some are worth avoiding, and all are worth respecting.

Approaching these beings with respect and seeking consent for building a partnership is, then, the foundation of building a mutually supportive relationship, and respect also gives them a good sense of who and what you are.

Navigating Faery Relations

When one goes on a journey it is helpful to have a guide and the path to Faeryland is no different. To uncover clues about who might be willing to help us on our path, we turn to an old Welsh myth, recorded in the medieval period:

Pwyll's Descent from Branch 1 of Y Mabinogi

(Version from "Pagan Portals; Gods and Goddesses of Wales" by Halo Quin)

A long time ago in his court of Arbeth, Pwyll, Prince of Dyfed, heard the call to go hunting in Glyn Cuch. And hunting he went. Late in the day he became separated from his companions and, as the sun began to dip in the sky, he cast about for them. Suddenly he spotted a white stag, darting through the trees. Unearthly hounds were chasing it, their baying like a howling storm in the distance. He made chase and caught up with the hunt just as the hounds took the stag down, their white coats and red tipped ears flashing in the light. Pwyll called the hounds off and leapt from his horse to take the antlers for himself.

As his knife touched the still-warm fur, a shadow fell across the stag. Pwyll looked up to see a great, proud man on a dappled grey horse, wearing brown-grey hunting gear and a hunting horn.

"I know who you are," Said the huntsman, "but I will not greet you as you have done me a dishonour."

Pwyll, however, did not know who the huntsman was and could not see what dishonour there could be, but he was a good man and offered to make it right if he could.

The huntsman explained;

"I have never seen such a discourteous act as to drive another's hounds from their kill and steal it for their own."

"I beg your pardon, but I am the lord of this land," responded Pwyll, "and so the stag belonged to me long before your hounds caught it."

"In my land I am a crowned King in my own right. I am Arawn, king of Annwn".

Now a king can pull rank on a lord regardless, but Annwn is the Otherworld of Wales and Pwyll knew now that the King before him not only had a higher rank than he, but was also much older, much more powerful, and had much more right to be hunting in the wildwood. Pwyll bowed deeply to Arawn.

Arawn set Pwyll a task to make things right; he must travel to the Otherworld to slay Hafgan, an otherworldly king who was terrorising Arawn's subjects.

"But how can I kill him?" Pwyll asked.

"Like so." Arawn replied, "I will make with you a strong bond of friendship. I will make you look like me, and I like you, so that no one will know the difference. In my guise you will rule Annwn, and the fairest lady you have ever seen will sleep with you each night in my chamber. A year from tonight Hafgan and I have sworn to meet by the ford. You must meet him there in my place and strike him just one mortal blow, and one blow only. When we fought last, I struck him twice and the second healed him and now I can do him no damage at all."

Pwyll agreed, for he wished to make things right, and Arawn showed him the way to his court. He cast a spell to make himself appear as Pwyll, and Pwyll appear as Arawn, and they returned to each other's lands.

Pwyll found that the Queen was indeed the fairest woman he had ever seen, and it was true that no-one saw through the magic of Arawn, so the whole court thought Pwyll was their lord, including the Queen. She was not only the fairest, but also the most down-to-earth, gracious and interesting lady he had ever had the opportunity to speak to. The moment they retired to bed, however, he turned his back and refused to speak to her or touch her, for he was not who she thought he was. Each day passed the same, and each night as well.

At the appointed time Pwyll went to meet Hafgan, and he struck just one mortal blow, as instructed.

"Ha, chieftain," Cried Hafgan, recognising that this, somehow, was not Arawn, "What right do you have to kill me? I had no quarrel with you? But as you have begun my death, I ask you to finish me quickly."

Pwyll lowered his head. "I may repent for what I have done, but I will not slay you now."

Hafgan was carried from the place to die and Pwyll sent out Arawn's people to gather oaths of allegiance from all the lords in the land. By midday the next day, the whole of Annwn was united under Arawn.

Pwyll met Arawn that evening as agreed and Arawn declared that Pwyll would always be a friend of Annwn. When he returned home to his wife, she was surprised at the affection he showed her. It was then that Arawn truly knew what kind of man Pwyll was, and he told the Queen all that had happened.

Pwyll, in turn, found that Arawn had ruled so well that he had made the kingdom of Dyfed an even better place than it had been before. They became such good friends that they were often sending each other gifts, and Arawn and his wife named their new friend Pwyll Pen Annwn, which means Pwyll, Head of Annwn.

The Faery Hounds

Animals feature heavily in faery lore, the white stag or doe often appears to lead the traveller into unexpected situations, the glittering hounds of Arawn and the Thomas' Queen's magical horse show them to hold sway over wild, magical forces. Faery beings are usually distinguished in some way, often by their colouring or their beauty, and in many cases faery animals are white, with red tipped ears. They lead the way through the gates to the otherworld or carry the beings of the otherworld to our realm. They offer their help and guidance to good people in many stories.

Though missing in the ballad, the earlier "romance" of *Thomas the Rhymer* describes the Queen as having hounds in the same way Arawn does. Given the time these were written this may be an indication of status, or their ability to control wild magic, or a reference to the Wild Hunt which is said to hunt down oath breakers on certain nights. For our purposes however, we can leave aside questions of symbolism and meet the hounds on their own terms.

As I developed the material for this book I worked closely with the hounds as they had offered to be a guiding, protective force for those that read and engage, and so I offer this next practice as an introduction for you, should you need one. These are powerful spirit beings who protect the beings who move between their world and ours, and so they can do the same for us. As always, treat them with respect and care, and without entitlement, and they will support you on this stage of your journey.

Practice 6. Meeting the Hounds (as protectors)

When we work with or contact spirits, we are allowing ourselves to become aware of a part of reality which we often ignore. It is easiest to reach this awareness through deep relaxation and trance-states. Trance states are natural states of mind that happen on a daily basis and are deliberately used in many cultures to facilitate healing and spirit-work. Certain rhythms are known to induce trance in the human brain and so the drum is often used to conjure trance, but you can also relax into it by focusing on your breathing for a few minutes and letting your mind relax. Pathworkings work like stories to guide us through specific experiences, so allow yourself to experience the following as an immersive story. If you'd like an academic exploration of the place of visionary experiences in folkloric spaces see Emma Wilby, *Cunning Folk and Familiar Spirits*.

Before you begin, get comfortable in front of your altar. If you can, lighting a candle is helpful. You can rest your gaze on the flame as you pay attention to your breathing to help you relax and enter a trance. Read through the following pathworking and fix the instructions in your mind. You can record it for yourself if that helps but be sure to give plenty of time between instructions for things to unfold. If you are able to drum for yourself then I highly recommend it, or if staying focussed whilst staying still is a challenge for you, you can also rock, stand and sway, tap your thighs or toes, or whatever you need to support your journey.

Set your intention to meet the protective, guiding, Faery Hounds, and then begin.

Pathworking One

Allow yourself to relax and breathe gently but deeply.

Imagine a protective golden light flowing around you and wrapping you in an egg of light.

Feel a mist rise from the earth and surround you.

The mists of Faeryland open before you onto three paths. One broad and bright, one thorny and narrow, and one with an abundance of plants growing either side. This is the path to Faeryland.

Imagine yourself moving through the mist onto the path to Faeryland. The path is not too wide and not too narrow. You can hear rivers roaring in the distance. The mist swirls around you, parting just enough that you can see the path you are to travel along. What lines the path? Which plants? Rocks? Trees?

Up ahead you see the path reaches a clearing, in the clearing is a small lake, shining silver. As you sit down beside the lake you find a silver horn on the lakeshore beside you. It has a vine of small golden roses engraved round the rim. Place it to your lips and blow, knowing that it's sound will call the Hounds of Faery to you.

A pack of Hounds, white with red tipped ears, splash out of the lake, happy to see you. They've been waiting for you.

They gather around you and greet you. Greet them in return.

Spend some time with them now.

When you are ready, ask them if they will protect and help guide you in this work.

Then ask if they would like you to do anything for them.

Eventually it will be time for you to leave, say farewell to the Hounds.

One or two may follow you home to look after you, but the rest return to the lake as you leave the clearing.

Follow the path back to where the paths began.

As you reach the place where you arrived in this land the mists swirl around you and carry you (and any hounds that followed you) back to your body, back to the world in which you live your daily life. Make notes on your experiences and eat something to reconnect with your normal state of awareness.

Repeat this pathworking a few times to get comfortable using pathworkings, meet the hounds and get to know them. Once you are comfortable with it you can add in the following piece to meet a faery being who is happy to work as your guide on this journey.

Practice 7. Meeting a Faery Guide
This pathworking builds on the journey you have taken to meet the Hounds, taking the same route but then allowing the Hounds to lead you onwards.

Pathworking Two
Allow yourself to relax and breathe gently but deeply.

Imagine a protective golden light flowing around you and wrapping you in an egg of light.

Feel a mist rise from the earth and surround you.

The mists of Faeryland open before you onto three paths. One broad and bright, one thorny and narrow, and one with an abundance of plants growing either side. This is the path to Faeryland.

Imagine yourself moving through the mist onto the path to Faeryland. The path is not too wide and not too narrow. You can hear rivers roaring in the distance. The mist swirls around you, parting just enough that you can see the path you are to travel along. What lines the path? Which plants? Rocks? Trees?

Up ahead you see the path reaches a clearing, in the clearing is a small lake, shining silver. As you sit down beside the lake you find a silver horn on the lakeshore beside you. It has a vine of small golden roses engraved round the rim. Place it to your lips and blow, knowing that it's sound will call the Hounds of Faery to you.

A pack of Hounds, white with red tipped ears, splash out of the lake, happy to see you. They've been waiting for you.

They gather around you and greet you. Greet them in return. Ask them to lead you to your Guide for this work. As one, the hounds lead you to another path leading from this clearing and you follow them along it, through soft green mists that swirl across the way.

Up ahead you see a figure in the mists. This is your Guide. Approach them with the willingness to work with them, to learn from each other, to perhaps become friends. Approach with respect, they've volunteered to be your guide in this land.

When you reach them, introduce yourself and ask what you may call them.

Spend some time with them. They may just want to talk, they may offer you advice, or they may take you further along the path and show you some part of the land. If, at any point, you don't feel ready for something they suggest, thank them and say so.

Eventually it will be time for you to leave, say farewell to your guide, thank them and follow the path back to the clearing, where you say farewell to the hounds, and then, again, back to where the paths began.

As you reach the place where you arrived in this land the mists swirl around you and carry you back to your body, back to the world in which you live your daily life. Make notes on your experiences and eat something to reconnect with your normal state of awareness.

Again, practice travelling to meet your guide until you are comfortable with it. It will sometimes take a few goes to really get a good sense of success, but it will come.

Integration

You might choose to add images of your guide and the hounds to your altar to give them space in your work and revisit the pathworkings as you feel the need arise. Continue your research and keeping notes on what you find.

Do try to get outside, perhaps visit your hawthorn tree, at least once a day to tune into a sense of the presence of faery spirits or enchantment. If you can't go far from home, sitting in a doorway or by an open window is also helpful. This has the benefit of being a "liminal" space, which is good for meeting faeries. Otherwise, spend time with a picture or representation of a hawthorn tree at your altar. Make a note of how you feel and when – which days and times – you do this. Over time you might notice a pattern of when is a better time for you.

Questions to Ponder

What is your understanding of "trance"?

How did it feel to use the pathworkings?

What does it mean to act with respect? Towards spirits? Towards the land? Towards the Fair Folk?

How did the Hounds appear to you, and if different to described, why might this be?

Once you've encountered the Hounds – what do you think they might represent?

What motivations do you have for contacting spirits such as faeries and building (perhaps working) relationships with them?

Chapter 3

Beginning the Journey

"But you must go with me now, Thomas,
True Thomas, you must go with me,
For you must serve me seven years,
Through well or woe as may chance to be."

She turned about her milk-white steed,
And took True Thomas up behind,
And aye whene'er her bridle rang,
The steed flew swifter than the wind.

We began this book with learning some context, making space for faery magic and meeting our guides, now we follow the path that is opening before us.

How Can We Recognise Faeries?

I spent a great deal of my childhood actively looking for faeries, and getting very frustrated that I didn't see a single one. I knew they were there, however, because I could *feel* them. This is a very important distinction, when someone talks about *seeing* faeries they generally don't mean with their physical eyes. Seeing spirits is often more about sensing them in some way. It can be a feeling, a sound like the faery queen's bells, an impression, a particular but inexplicable scent. It can be a vision, but it doesn't have to be. In fact, straining to physically see a spirit can get in the way of sensing them at all! The Fair Folk are also traditionally not keen on being stared at, which is completely understandable – who is? – and will often disguise themselves so as not to be easily spotted. In Wales one form for the Tylwyth Teg is the humble hedgehog, purposefully traveling the edges of the paths at dusk and into the night. We can understand this literally, or we can take the sceptical view that people caught sight of movement in the gloom and mistook it for a spirit, and when it resolved itself to be a hedgehog, they assumed this was the shape a spirit had taken. We can also come to a possible truth somewhere between the two – perhaps sometimes it's one, sometimes it's the other, but sometimes it is that the spirits slip into our line of sight through the edges of uncertainty in our understanding, or they "ride" or "possess" other beings to move through the physical world. It can be tricky to recognise when something was our imagination or a mistake, as opposed to a genuine appearance, but practice helps.

What we're going to do in this chapter is to take steps towards getting to know the feeling of faery magic so we can recognise it when we come across faery magic on our journey.

Tolkien described faerie as a state of being, and any being or place or atmosphere that evokes this enchantment and wonder inherent in faery magic carries faerie. I call it enchantment. When we are enchanted, we feel ourselves open up in wonder or awe at the world, and in these moments, we can feel the otherworldly magic of the fae. This works for other kinds of magic and spirits also, so using the tales to pinpoint the indicators of fae-specific magic is very helpful.

Faeries are liminal, on the edges of our world, so the best places to find them are in-between places. The edge of a forest, the sand between land and sea, doorways. And the best times are the same; dusk or dawn, midsummer's eve, the changing of the seasons, your birthday. Water acts as a portal to otherworlds, so the edge of water at dusk or dawn is perfect. Wherever you go, please do take sensible precautions for physical safety and choose somewhere within your limitations. Aside from anything else, anxiety about danger is an obstacle we don't need when learning to sense faeries.

Many fairy tales begin with someone entering the forest and

going beyond the familiar human landscape of daily life. Over time you will find faery magic in cities and towns too, and they certainly have a presence in many homes, but for now, choose somewhere that feels like it might be a doorway to Faeryland.

Practice 8. Entering Waking Trance States

Choose a space to visit that feels enchanted to you, or find a picture of such a place to place on your altar if getting outside is not possible. If you are inside, imagine yourself in the place you have chosen. Take an offering of some milk and honey and nice bread, or similar. I like to read, recite, or sing them a faery themed poem, which also tunes me into them, as well as inviting them to be near. Choose wisely. Get comfortable. Read the following visualisation and then imagine your way through it a few times, until you feel happy with it.

Breathe deeply and calmly. Allow any tensions to drain from your body and sink into the earth. Keep breathing and relaxing for as long as you need to.

Invite the hounds of faery to watch over you, and your guide to be present.

Now imagine all of your attention is a golden light in your head, spread out around you. Notice how far it spreads.

Breathe calmly and with each breath imagine it pulling back into your skull until it becomes a golden ball of light. Take your time.

When it is focussed, keep breathing and imagine it sinking down, through your neck, past your heart and into your belly. From there it spreads out like the surface of a pool around you, until it is a comfortable size. Be aware of the edges of your attention at the level of your belly and how that opens you up to a different kind of awareness of the world.

Make your offering to the fae.

Relax and allow a feeling of enchantment to surround you.

When you are ready, let the feeling of faery dissipate, breathe your attention back into the ball in your belly, allow it to rise back into your skull and relax outwards into what is normal and comfortable for you.

Make note of any impressions you received, of how it felt to experience enchantment, if it reminded you of anything and so on. Eat something, drink some water, thank your guide and the hounds and bid them a fond farewell.

This exercise is a practice to get us out of the mindset where we think and try too hard and into a space where we can feel from our gut, which is much more responsive to any kind of magic than our head is. I learned it from Reclaiming Witchcraft under the name "Dropped and Open Attention", a process developed by Anne Hill from a practice in aikido, and have woven in the faery enchantment aspects, but you can practice the gathering and dropping of attention in many different situations.

Hopefully you have a sense of what faery magic might feel like now, if not, repeat this exercise again and don't worry about getting it *right* or forcing the experience. These things can take time.

Practice 9. Taking this Further – getting to know places, your guide, the hounds

When you do get a sense for enchantment, then see if you can be aware of when this feeling might show up at other times in your life. What kinds of places or times remind you of this feeling? What kinds of foods, smells, plants, activities and so on, feel enchanted to you?

Use the dropped and open technique to gently bring yourself into a receptive state – remembering to ask the Faery hounds to protect you – and test the feeling at different places and in different situations where you feel safe to do so. If it feels like a bad idea, trust your instincts. You can also use it as a framework for spending time getting to know your faery Guide and making friends with the Faery Hounds.

Reciprocity and Offerings

The tale of Pwyll's descent into Annwn also holds other clues for us on how to behave in our work. As in *Thomas the Rhymer*, where the queen insists on being recognised for who she is, Arawn is only respected when he is correctly recognised. Respect and recognition, dealing with these beings as the beings they are rather than as archetypes or ideas, is central to this work.

Other things highlighted by Pwyll's tale include:

The idea of reciprocity

Lack of greed (e.g. Pwyll doesn't take advantage of Arawn's wife)

Importance of following instructions (e.g. in order to slay Hafgan)

Different rules in different worlds

Offerings

As creatures that eat, drink, build, create and so on, we use a lot of resources. We can also find ourselves receiving help and support from the otherworld if the spirits consider us to have shown our worth. One way of making sure we give back and avoid a one-sided friendship is to make offerings. But what kind of offerings do they like? In the stories food is generally welcome, clothing most often is not.

Often the stories where clothing is offered describe the faery as being offended that we thought them unpresentable enough that they needed new clothes, or so excited by them and immersed in their own vanity that they dance off, but I suggest that another issue is at play. Food left or put outside can feed the earth as well as honouring the spirits by showing an awareness of the need for reciprocity. The land is where the fair folk live, so caring for the land is caring for their (and our) home. Clothing and other such items often do not break down in the same way so cannot do this. Clothes in particular also assume that faery nature is so much like ours that they need protection from the elements of which they are a part... you wouldn't give an umbrella to a raincloud, would you? That would be like telling the raincloud that it is bad to be rained on, so its fundamental existence is bad! Alongside this, all living things need nourishment, but only humans wear clothes and the faeries are not human, so to give them a gift that assumes they are firstly limits them and secondly ignores who they are. In short, give gifts of things *they* will like.

On the other hand, there is a tradition of giving coins and metal objects to bodies of water – think of wishing wells. Now, the fae certainly don't need money like we do but metal is of the earth and we invest a lot of energy and importance into money so perhaps it is a good demonstration of sacrifice on our part, if given in appropriate places.

Offerings must be appropriate, then, to the spirit and to the place it is given, with an awareness of the impact it can have on other beings. I try never to give dark chocolate in places a dog might snaffle it as it can be very bad for dogs. Songs sung to the trees leave no waste, and paper offerings are better on an indoor altar or in a fire. You can also make offerings of donations of time or money to a local environmental group or similar. Do state out loud to the spirits that the offerings are for them, even if you have to whisper it, so they know for certain.

Traditional European offerings include; milk and honey, bread, music, dance, a space at the dinner table on special occasions, coins in wishing wells, incense smoke on an altar. What offerings do you see being made and accepted in your local faery lore?

Practice 10. Making Offerings

Think of three offerings, one for your altar, one for water and one for land. Consider carefully; where will you be making this offering? Who are you making it to? What is the purpose of making it? And, as a result, what will it be? Gather your offerings together and, at appropriate times for you, go make them.

Local Landspirits

The fae are land-based spirits in that they are of the land, as we are, but we have touched upon the fact that not all spirits of the land are faeries. Although there are some who travel long distances – as described in tales of "Trooping Fae", "The Wild Hunt" and faery allies who travel with their humans – they are often associated with specific locations and certain caves, rocks or trees are known to be their homes. They also have had a relationship with humans for a long time, so it is important to research the interactions already known to local humans. The spirits of any land also include the spirits of the dead of that land, and so you will encounter the dead when seeking out faery contact. This is perfectly fine, but as a result it is helpful to understand the cultures who have lived on the land you inhabit for two reasons: firstly, the faery spirits here will have preferences and taboos which the previous inhabitants have learned (or negotiated), making your job easier when you approach your local faeries, and secondly, if you come across the ancestor of a people who you don't belong to, you will have a better idea of how to approach them with respect, and perhaps gain another ally in the process! Thomas the Rhymer, for example, is a human spirit, one of the dead, who works closely with the faery realm and often acts as an intermediary between us and them. Perhaps when you are seeking faeries you will find a similar human spirit who would be willing to help you in that pursuit, or others, and knowing how to show them respect gets you off to a good start. Again, think of it as like visiting another country; if you understand the customs, you can interact better with the people there and make new friends, and just as the customs in Germany differ from the customs in Spain, the customs in the German Otherworld differ from the customs in the Spanish Otherworld.

Practice 11. Learning About Local Spirits

If you haven't already, pop into your local library (or investigate online) and see if there are any books on folktales or folklore for your area. Begin to read about the history of the place, the people who came before and their relationship to the landscape and spirits. See if you can identify the sacred plants for spirit contact, and the places which are considered to be home to the spirits. Make a note of whether they are considered to be friendly or not! Some will be places to avoid, others are places to make contact.

Integration

Revisit the pieces from Chapters 1 and 2 and see if there's anything you'd like to repeat. You might like to experiment with doing the "Dropped and Open Attention" exercise before one of the pathworkings, to see how that changes things.

You might find something to represent the local spirits to add to your altar, or perhaps a bowl or plate that can live on your altar or somewhere in your home to hold offerings. These might be offerings to the spirits of your home or to the faeries in general. Consider how you might dispose of indoor offerings respectfully.

Take an offering to your hawthorn tree, or make an offering in your garden or at your altar if you can't get outside. Continue spending time connecting with the outside if possible.

You could also write a little about your experiences of encountering faeries, or Tolkien's sense of faerie/enchantment.

Questions to Ponder

What does it mean to "see" a faery or other spirit?
Why might you pursue enchantment?

What kind of offerings might you choose to make?

How would you distinguish between the different types of land spirits in your locale?

Chapter 4

Crossing the Rivers

For forty days and forty nights
He wade through red blood to the knee,
And he saw neither sun nor moon,
But heard the roaring of the sea.

O they rode on, and further on,
Until they came to a garden green:
"Light down, light down, ye lady free,
Some of that fruit let me pull to thee."

"O no, O no, True Thomas," she says,
"That fruit must not be touched by thee,
For all the plagues that are in hell
Light on the fruit of this country."

"But I have a loaf here in my lap,
Likewise a bottle of claret wine,
And now 'ere we go farther on,
We'll rest a while, and ye may dine."

Faeryland is often described as being found across the water or through the forest, it is another realm, reached by traveling across or through another element. Though Pwyll reached Annwn through the forests, and later met a Faery Queen (Rhiannon, notably; the gods of Wales often blur the lines between deity and faery) who appeared from the mists while he sat on a magical mound, Faeryland is often reached through water, whether across a river, as for Thomas, over the ocean, down a well or through a millpond.

In each case Faeryland is *on the other side* of somewhere. It is not part of our everyday consciousness and so needs to be marked by a transition. Water or darkness are good mediums for this because they soothe our minds and allow us to shift our brainwaves to those more conducive to an awareness of otherworldly magic, enchantment, or spirits.

The tale of Mother Holla is a good example of this kind of travel-between and interactions with an otherworldly being, and so it can offer us clues as to what to do once we reach an awareness of faery magic…

Story: Mother Holla

Once, not so long ago, there was a widow with two daughters. The youngest daughter was clever and hardworking, but the eldest was lazy. Even so, the widow loved her best.

The youngest daughter would work hard, often spinning until her fingers bled, and still it was not enough to gain a kind word from the widow. One day she was spinning by the well and the blood began to drip from her fingers. She dipped the spindle into the well to clean it but it slipped from her hands and fell into the water.

Her mother was furious and sent her back to the well to retrieve the spindle. The girl had no choice but to dive into the cold water, where the shock knocked her out.

When she awoke, the girl found herself in a different land, on the edge of a wood, with a cottage just through the trees. She walked towards the cottage and came across a bread oven. From inside the oven the bread cried out:

"Take me out! Before I burn!" And so she did.

A little further ahead was an apple tree, heavy with apples.

"Shake the apples from my branches," called the tree, "before they rot!" And so she did.

Soon she reached the cottage, where an old woman was waiting and watching what had happened.

"Would you like to stay with me awhile?" The old lady asked. "I've

much work that I need help with. If you do the work well, I will make sure you are very happy."

The girl agreed to stay, thinking that she certainly did not know how to return home even if she wanted to. The woman invited her in, gave her a good meal and a place by the embers to sleep. In the morning she instructed the girl to shake out her bedcovers every morning.

"You must be sure to shake them out well," she said, "for when the feathers fly here it snows upon the earth, and the snow allows the trees and flowers and crops to sleep the sleep they need. I am Mother Holla"

The girl, dutifully shook the covers until feathers flew and it snowed upon the earth. She did every task asked of her with care and had, in return, the best meals she had ever tasted and the best rest she had ever known. She even had time to herself. As the days and weeks went by, Mother Holla began to teach the girl things that might be useful, and the girl was very happy.

Eventually, however, she began to think of home and grew homesick. She went and told Mother Holla that she wished to go home.

"You have served me well," Mother Holla said, "so I shall take you home myself."

She led the girl to a wide gateway and as the girl passed through it, she was covered in gold from head to toe. Mother Holla handed her the spindle which has been lost in the well and sent her home, to arrive back only a moment after she'd left!

You can imagine that the widow was excited to see the gold, but she still scolded the girl, and when she found out what had happened, she sent the lazy daughter to get gold as well!

The lazy girl pricked her finger, smeared blood on the spindle and threw it into the well before diving in after it. Unlike her sister, however, when she heard the oven ask for help, she passed it by, leaving the bread to burn. The apples she left on the tree – all except one which she plucked for herself.

Like her sister, Mother Holla invited her in and for the first day the lazy girl did everything to the best of her ability. But the second day she only shook the covers until a few feathers flew, and by the third day she only did tasks at all when she knew Mother Holla was watching.

After a week she told Mother Holla she was homesick and had to go home, so Mother Holla took her to the gate, and the girl was pleased. But, instead of gold, Mother Holla's gate covered the lazy girl in sticky tar, and even when she got home, she could never get it off.

Mother Holla's tale is one in which the well water, is a portal to the otherworld. This well water is water that comes from under the ground, so it also contains chthonic properties; aspects of the hidden, the non-human, the deep.

When we approach Faeryland or the otherworld, we need to maintain an awareness that we are changing our consciousness for one that is not part of the everyday. We slip deeper into a relaxed state. Stories often indicate that this happens during sleep, as when True Thomas is dreaming under the Hawthorn, during a repetitive task, such as spinning or walking through the forest, or when we are being deeply creative or focused, as when playing music or hunting. These are all instances where our brainwaves change into more relaxed and aware states than our everyday, stressed, survival mode allows for. That the subsequent events which occur during these trances are not commented on by the protagonist as strange reminds us that these states of mind are perfectly natural.

The first girl encounters three requests for help – the oven, the tree and from Mother Holla herself – and she fulfils them without hesitation. She is willing to give of herself, to act as part of the whole and support the world around her. The fact that normally inanimate objects speak indicate that this is not the everyday world we are accustomed to, but somewhere else, and so the rules are different, but her kind, respectful attitude will help her when she returns, just as it does for Pwyll in Annwn.

The gift of gold when she returns home is an indication of what is possible for her. The attitude of the lazy daughter, however, leads to the opposite result and a permanent reminder that she treated the beings of the otherworld with disdain.

Housework as a Magical Act

When the first daughter meets Mother Holla, we already know she is hardworking, but it is housework she must do to prove her value to the otherworldly lady. Aside from the proof of character, however, housework has many other magical applications.

Firstly, cleaning is a way of exercising magical control over a space. This leads to a greater power over which energies or spirits can enter your home. By cleaning it you claim the space and make it your own. It also helps you to strengthen your will, which is useful when dealing with non-corporeal beings, by strengthening your sense of your ability to manifest change in reality.

Secondly, cleanliness is healthier, on all levels. If you have less clutter and mess, your mental health improves and you are less distracted by additional stimulation in your space. If you have cleaned a space then you are less likely to get ill in it. And if you have physically cleaned then you will have shifted the energetic, magical parts of the space and helped move stuck, stagnant energies. You can also weave in prayers and magical herbs, oils or waters to support this energetic cleansing.

Thirdly you make space for the beings and energies you wish to invite into your home, it is like making your home welcoming for guests. In doing so you demonstrate care for your environment, and a respectful attitude towards both the space and your guests.

Full disclosure: cleaning is not one of my strong points. My home is rarely up to the standard of cleanliness that my mother would keep their home. For some people it can be a real struggle to maintain expected standards of cleanliness, due to disabilities, time, or other factors. If that's you, don't panic. I do what I can, when I can. I keep my space as close to the standard that I am comfortable with, and when I do certain cleaning activities I'll dedicate it to my energetic guests, for example, when I sweep the floor or make the bed, I might dedicate the act and the energy it to Mother Holla. We each do what we can, and we need to honour that in ourselves. (However, if you just can't be bothered and let things slide through wilful neglect, then recognise that and see if you consider making your home welcoming to the beings you wish to work with enough motivation to do better.) With that in mind, here are a couple of things you can add in to your cleaning to make it more effective on an energetic level.

Practice 12. Cleaning Magic

Have a look around your home, however big or small that is. Does it feel clean and tidy? Does it feel welcoming? What one thing can you do today to make it feel a little better? Could your floor do with a sweep? Are there dishes you could wash? Does your desk need organising? Pick one task that you can do now.

A good way to cleanse a space energetically is to use herbs for cleansing. Smudging is probably one of the best known practices involving herbs for cleansing. Smudging is specifically a Native American practice involving a tightly tied bundle of dried sage, and wafting the smoke through the space to clear the space in a specific ritual. It is best, however, to not use white sage unless this is part of your family heritage as using actual white sage is culturally appropriative. It is also environmentally damaging as that specific kind of sage is very hard to grow outside of its original area, and has been over-harvested for consumers. You can, however, use garden sage for very much the same effect, or burn dried mugwort (Nordic) or heather (British) as a dried herb bundle, or an incense on charcoal disks instead. Smoke is not always practical however, and a water wash can be used instead.

Make a cup of tea with a little bit of loose sage, rosemary and thyme (a palmful of fresh herbs or a spoonful of dried).
Strain out the herbs and put them in the compost or under a hedge or tree so they can return to the soil.
Add a teaspoon of sea salt.
Add this to your floor washing water before mopping, or sprinkle it round the space, flicking it with your fingers or using a sprig of fresh rosemary. Make sure you get some in the corners of each room, and in windows and doors.

As you do so you can use a prayer for blessing, such as this one from the collection of Scottish poems and prayers *Carmina Gadelica, Vol. 1*:

God bless the house,
From site to stay,
From beam to wall,
From end to end,
From ridge to basement,
From balk to roof-tree,
From found to summit,
Found and summit.

(Note: you can amend the words to suit your practice and beliefs. The important aspect here is that you are intending and asking for blessing on the house. As a pagan I might substitute "Gods" for "God", or perhaps "Mother Holla", for example.)

Whenever using herbs, do take care to research exactly what you are using, and check for contraindications and allergies for yourself and others you share your home with. It is also, obviously, important to practice fire safety if you are burning anything, and to be careful where you spray water if using washes. Common sense is your friend!

Faery Mounds and Holy Wells

Hopefully by now you will have come across mentions of sites in your area which are known to be home to the fae. They are often linked with mounds – unusual hills or burial mounds – lone trees, unusual stones, and bodies of water, like Mother Holla's well. Both are considered to be gateways to Faeryland, or homes to the Fair Folk.

Hills considered to be "Faery Mounds" are often Iron Age (or similar) burial mounds, and certain tales have instructions for reaching Faeryland by walking anti-clockwise round them three times, or doing the same in a graveyard. This links the Fair Folk with the dead, both are beings that are similar to us, can be helpful or dangerous (guardian ancestors or angry ghosts, for example) and who live in the lands below the everyday world. We bury our dead within the land, and by doing so, perhaps this opens an entrance to the subterranean lands (as the faery scholar Robert Kirk called them) of the Fae. Burial mounds sometimes have entrances which we can physically walk into the earth through, so when those physical entrances have closed, perhaps the otherworldly door remains. Mounds of a similar shape and size to burial mounds may well have served as burial chambers once upon a time, or maybe the Fae are mimicking those liminal spaces by encouraging them to grow up from the land itself. In either case, it is said that if you sit upon a faery mound – just as Pwyll did – at the right time, you may well find yourself met by a Faery.

Wells, lakes, springs and other bodies of water have similar properties. They lead into the land. Springs bubble up from somewhere mysterious, wells fill from unseen sources. Lakes are mysterious places with unknown activity beneath the surface... As such they are also gateways into the subterranean, and inner, lands. In many stories faeries come out of the water, or humans enter Faeryland by going beneath the surface. In the Lady of the Millpond, a story from Ceredigion collected by Peter Stevenson, the faery lady appears from the millpond, and takes her human lover into Faeryland down through the waters. In Mother Holla, of course, the girls travel in both directions, but we don't see Mother Holla in our world. It is notable that Thomas was resting on the banks of a river when the Faery Queen came to find him. Perhaps she rose from the waters? And, of course, they crossed rivers to get to her country of Elfland.

Practice 13. Visiting a Faery Gateway

Look through your research and pick out one of the places you have found, perhaps a mound or a well, or think about somewhere which you feel might belong to the fae. If possible, visit that location this week and take a suitable offering. It is good to do this at a liminal time such as dawn, dusk, midday or midnight, or on certain days like the summer or winter solstices, as those are times the veil between the world are said to be thinnest, but this is not always practical.

Invite your guide to accompany you, and the faery Hounds to guide and protect you. When you leave your offering, if it feels like the right thing to do, make a request for a sign from the faeries of that place to show they've received your gift and see what happens in the following days. Messages can be quite subtle or very obvious, but they are almost always presented in a way that you could explain it away, using the things around you. You might see an unusual phrase or image on the side of a lorry, for example, or overhear something that sounds out of place as you pass people talking under the Hawthorn trees in the local park. Allow yourself to notice these things – which Carl Jung called synchronicities – that are slightly out of place and seem to be responding to your request. These are messages from the other world.

The Fae and the Dead

In other stories of Mother Holla it is said that the spirits of lost children live in her well, and she cares for them. Sometimes she is described as leading a "Faery Ride" – a parade of fae beings that travels across the land, sometimes known as a form of the Wild Hunt – which is strongly associated with the spirits of the dead.

There is a long history of the dead and the fae being related. Both the dead and the Fae are said to live under the earth or in mounds, both their lands can be reached by traveling West, over the water, in Irish tales. In Norse mythology the Alfar (Elves) are spoken of as both male ancestors and as land-based spirits, so the lines between the two types of spirit are blurred. In many fairy tales where someone ends up in Faeryland, they meet dead friends or relatives (who often warn the visitor of danger or help them return home).

This connection makes sense when we realise that our bodies are of the earth and we will return to the land which fed and housed us, leaving our spirits in a similar position to faery beings who are land spirits, i.e. connected to the earth and in a different world to the one we live in in day to day life. As in Chapter 3 I suggested researching the local, historical cultures of your area and learning both how they interacted with the fae and how to greet them respectfully, here I recommend that you continue this research. Look for both information on the human cultures, and the non-human lives who live here, and whose spirits are also present in the otherworld.

You can also look to your own ancestors, those who are connected to you by blood and those who have inspired you. Who do you know and respect of your ancestors, if any? Which individuals who have passed on inspire you, or created traditions or works that have shaped your life? Consider authors, artists, religious leaders, dancers, revolutionaries... anyone who has had an impact on your life. Would you like to work with any of these individuals in the work you do? Do you think there are any who would like to support you in your faery workings?

Consider also the non-human dead, perhaps there are creatures who are extinct from your local land who inspire you and you feel would be good to work with.

A metaphysical thought to explore: In Chapter 2 I mentioned that the realm of the dead is often considered to be the lower realm, where the realm of faerie is more on a level with the middle realm, where now we see that there is overlap between the dead and the fae. This discrepancy can be resolved in a number of ways. Firstly, we can recognise that there are different aspects to the dead, just as there are to the fae, and the individual spirits, such as those met via mediumship are closer to us and our living realm than the Dead as a whole, that primordial energetic home of un-individuated spirits that once were alive but now are part of the powers behind existence. Secondly, we can consider the model of the realms or worlds as distinct layers as a massive oversimplification, and perhaps a series of intertwined spiralling nebulae would be a better image. And thirdly, most simply, we can accept that there is perhaps a paradox here, and that our desire to delineate and label limits the way in which we can talk and think about these things. They are useful models, and interesting to explore, but not necessarily hard and fast objective realities.

Practice 14. Ancestor Contemplation

If this work calls to you there are many strands to follow, but in the interests of showing respect to those spirits you might encounter, or who might be supporting your work, spend a little time with your journal writing about the idea of ancestors and the spirits of the dead.

Who do you know of your own blood ancestors? Do you want them in your life?

Who of the famous dead have shaped important parts of your life, directly or indirectly? Would you like to include them in your

honouring?
Who lived on the land before you did? Are there specific ways you can honour them that are appropriate to them and their culture?
Which non-human spirits lived here or impacted on your life? How can you honour them?
What stories about the dead of this land do you know?
Once you have your answers look it over. Do you need to do some research?

Gather together some images or objects that represent the individuals, cultures or species that feel important to you to include at this time. See if you can include these on your faery altar, or on a separate altar. Think back over the offerings section in Chapter 3 and consider might be an appropriate gift for these ancestors. A simple option is to leave a glass of fresh water for them every morning or evening, or to say a prayer or sing them a song. When I lived in shared accommodation with very little space, I used to keep certain items in a special box for my Beloved Dead, which I'd get out periodically and contemplate the stories and connections behind, and I would regularly make a cup of tea for my blood ancestors in a special teacup and place it on the windowsill.

Integration
When you go on your wanders, take little items you can leave as offerings in suitable places.

Continue meeting with your guide in pathworkings and seeing how that feels. Try it in outdoor places if you can, on faery mounds and suchlike. Try it in doorways and corridors – liminal spaces – and at your altar. Keep notes of when, where and what happens or how it feels in your journal. Look back over what you've done so far and see if you can spot any patterns.

What happens if you clean your house (or part of it) after doing the "Dropped and Open Attention" exercise from Chapter 3?

Visit your Hawthorn tree again or spend some time with its representation. Talk to it about what you're doing. Listen to/feel its response.

Questions to Ponder

Why might there be a connection between the faery folk and the dead?

What could/does it mean for your practice that they are connected?

How does care of your space and hospitality feature in your magical practice?

What do you think might cause faery gateways?

Chapter 5

Entering Faeryland

When he had eaten and drunk his fill,
"Lay down your head upon my knee,"
The lady said, "'ere we climb yon hill,
And I will show you fair things three."

"O see you not that narrow road,
So thick beset with thorns and briars?
That is the path of righteousness,
Though after it but few enquire."

"And see not you that broad broad road,
That lies across yon lillie leven?
That is the path of wickedness,
Though some call it the road to heaven."

"And see not you that bonny road,
Which winds about the fernie brae?
That is the road to fair Elfland,
Where you and I this night will go."

Though in many of folk tales the protagonist does not enter Faeryland but encounters the faeries here, it is also not unusual to hear of people stepping into a faery ring and dancing the night away with them, or being taken to their world. Thomas certainly fits into this category, as does the Midwife in the tale below.

Story: Faery Midwife

In a town not too far from here there lived a midwife who was very good at her job. One day she heard a knock at the door, and when she opened it a tall, handsome gentleman was there.

"My wife is having her baby," He explained, "will you help?"

The midwife immediately gathered her midwifery bag and her shawl and followed the gentleman down the road. He took a strange route and soon she found herself lost, as the path wound its way through the forest. Then they came to a grand house and the door opened silently. The gentleman rushed through the opulent hall and took the midwife straight to a beautiful chamber, where a woman in labour was on the bed.

The midwife set to work and eventually a beautiful baby was born.

As the woman lay, exhausted, the gentleman returned and handed the midwife a bottle of ointment as she was washing the baby.

"When he is clean," the gentleman said, "cover him thoroughly in this ointment, but be sure not to get any in your eyes."

The midwife thought it an odd instruction but did as she was told. Unfortunately, before she had a chance to wash her hands, she rubbed the sleep from one eye, and in went a smear of the ointment! Immediately the room changed. It was like looking at two different places, with her right eye she could still see the beautiful bedchamber, but with her left eye she found that it had become transformed into a damp cave, full of spirits. The bed was a pallet of straw. The mother and child, however, remained the same. The midwife gave a little gasp and the woman looked up sharply.

"What can you see?" She asked, knowing the answer from the midwife's confusion. "As you have helped me, let me help you in return. This place is under an enchantment to make it seem beautiful, and our ointment has let you see the truth. But you must not reveal to my husband that you can see through the magic. Please, return home and tell no-one."

The midwife nodded, silently, and moments later the gentleman returned. He looked very different now, with skin rough like tree bark and hair like vines.

"Come now, I will take you home." He commanded, and so he did.

A few years later the midwife saw the gentleman in the market, *moving quietly between the stalls and the other market patrons. In her excitement to know how the child was doing she called out to him. He looked up in surprise.*

"By which eye do you see me?" He asked her. She pointed, slowly, to her left eye. Without another word he pulled out a knife and plucked out her eye. Never again did she see him.

Rules and Taboos in Faery work

Faery ointment is a common feature of tales with the fae, for we so often cannot see past our everyday realm and need something to help us see their truth. In the tale of the midwife above we can see how she gains the ointment accidentally – it was not given to her directly, and so she should not have had it. The faeries are known as the Hidden Folk for several reasons, and one is that they prefer to have privacy, and to choose who they welcome into their family. However, if she had followed the instructions she was given, then she would have earned the ability to keep her faery sight. As in the tale of Pwyll's descent and Mother Holla, following instructions is shown to be key in dealing with the Hidden Folk, if they choose to show themselves. There are various taboos associated with the Fae throughout the tales, and these are worth considering.

Firstly, do not eat the food of Faeryland or you shall never leave. This makes sense as we are part of the land which we live upon, we consume the food from this world and it keeps us grounded and alive here. It stands to reason that this would be the same in Faeryland. However, there are exceptions to this, such as when the Faery Queen gives Thomas bread and wine, or in some versions, an apple.

Secondly, iron is often considered to be disliked by the faeries, although, conversely, they are said to like smiths and forges. Perhaps this is because smiths are transforming the iron, so there is magic happening here. Regardless, an iron nail or knife is known to be protection against unwanted faery influences, so it would be polite to avoid carrying iron when you are trying to build a relationship with them, or sensible to do so if you attract unwanted attention.

Thirdly, they often do not like to be thanked directly, though they appreciate a demonstration of appreciation. This may be connected to the importance of honesty – or of silence – in the stories. Faeries are said to never lie, though they can tell half-truths or withhold information, they will know if what you say does not match up with the truth, and so words of thanks without an action to accompany it may be seen as dishonest. Similarly, if one does not speak, one cannot lie. There is also the argument that a "thank you" is an acknowledgement that you are in their debt, and a favour of unspecified nature could potentially lead to trouble if they decide to call upon you.

Consider the taboos above, and the instructions and rules you may have noticed in your research. What do these things tell you about faery nature and the best way to interact with them?

Practice 15. Contemplating the Realms

Spend a bit of time contemplating the differences between faery folk and human folk, between their land and ours, that you've come across in your research and the texts shared in this book so far. What do those differences tell you about the kind of benefits that might be found in working with them? What about how or where Faeryland might be found? What do you imagine it would be like?

Requests

You may have noticed that visitors to Faeryland often get asked to perform certain tasks, alongside the things they must not do. In some versions of the ballad, Thomas is invited to become the Faery Queen's lover, Pwyll is asked to defeat an enemy that Arawn cannot, Mother Holla asks for help in keeping her home clean and doing the chores, the other beings the girl meets also ask for help with what they need, and the midwife is fetched because her help is required in the birthing of a child. Each of these actions are tangible, practical activities. This too shows us something of the nature of the Fae and what they might want from us.

We are embodied beings, which gives us great power in the physical realm. We can tend to plants so they grow better, clear blocked waterways so other animals can drink, care for each other and other animals, and support the literal journeying of other people between the worlds in birth and death. Even cleaning Mother Holla's house demonstrates a physical form of assistance which, presumably, makes life better for her, perhaps by sharing the work, or by making more space for her, or perhaps for other reasons.

Spirits are sometimes said to be envious of our physicality, connected to stories of them stealing human children (which may well have their roots in child mortality or disabilities but could then give rise to the thought that the Fair Folk are jealous of the embodied). If this envy is rooted in our power to move and shape the physical world, then perhaps that is what they want from us in a relationship. They can show us things beyond our knowledge, we can move things that they cannot touch. Perhaps they want something else from you specifically. The only way to know for sure, however, is to ask them directly.

Practice 16. Listening to the Fair Folk

Go outside if you can, preferably to a place you have identified as connected to the faery folk. If you can't, sit at your altar. Invite your Guide and the Faery Hounds to join you.

Make an offering as an invitation for the fae to join you and spend some time in contemplation. Ask them what they would like from you. Allow a response to arise. You might hear it, or you might get an image or impression, a feeling or a knowing that feels like it comes from them. If the request is one you can fulfil then make a pledge to do it, and if you can set a time limit on it then that is a good idea. If it is not one you can take on then explain that you cannot, and make a counter-offer which is aligned with what they've asked for. Wait for the response and if you get a feeling that this is the right task, do that.

If you don't get a response you're sure of then don't worry. Choose something which you feel they would appreciate and pledge to do that for them this time.

The tasks might seem pointless or silly, or it might feel weighty and important. It doesn't matter, in this time you are learning to listen and demonstrating that you can be taken at your word. Slowly you will find that you get a sense of the answer. Be aware that they have different sense of time to us, and of possibility and practicality. I was once asked to come play in some very deep water, which would have been dangerous to me. I declined. They didn't really understand, but they accepted my response and are still talking to me!

The Dream Realm

In many stories the dream realm is considered to be part of the spirit world, and so when we dream, perhaps we can step into Faeryland, or at least a part of the worlds where the Fae can visit us. It is often hard to get past the sceptical part of ourselves that wants to rationalise our experiences based on what is socially acceptable but as we fall asleep, we hand over control from our conscious mind to our instinctive, intuitive, creative selves so we can ask our dream selves to visit certain places or introduce us to certain beings if we wish. Then the trick is learning to bring the memories of the otherworld back from the dream realm into our conscious, waking world.

Dreaming can be thought of as stepping into another realm, traveling between the worlds, and so we can learn to travel to Faeryland by dreaming ourselves into it. If we cannot hold onto the gifts of our visits, however, they turn into leaves and dirt in our waking hands like faery gold taken without permission or respect.

Practice 17. Dreaming of Faeryland

To bring your visions home then, if you do not already keep a dream journal to record your dreams, I recommend that you start one. Everyone dreams and having a practice of immediately writing down what you have dreamed of will improve your dream recall. Just setting the intention to remember and having pen and paper handy will let your dreaming mind know that you value it, and encourage dream recall. You need to do this as soon as possible when you wake, however, and best is before you move too much as this seems to shake details away. Once you've gotten into the habit of writing them down, you will find that the path between the dreaming world and the waking world will become clearer and details are harder to bring back. It becomes like a path that gets easier as it is trodden down over time. You may find that this strengthens your ability to journey between the worlds and recall details of visions and visualisations in other ways as well.

Conversely, if you find you remember a lot of details, note down the main places, characters and occurrences, and anything which feels important, don't try to write down everything, as that will take you all day! (Trust me, I learned this the hard way…)

Once you have your dream journal up and running, when you go to bed you can ask for a dream from the faeries, whether on a specific theme or whatever they wish to share with you. As you drift off, keep your request in mind and, on waking, note down anything that felt fae to you. You can ask your guide to meet you in your dreams on specific nights and have conversations with them in dream time. They may not appear in the guise you are expecting, however, so be aware of recurring themes or appearances over several nights when you have requested their presence. Although it sounds simple, asking for a visit before you sleep and writing down your dreams the next morning really works.

Over the years I've found this has become a very effective way of making contact with faeries, and other spirits too, so I wish you many enjoyable dream-contacts!

Integration

Which taboos or requests have you found in your research? Have you found references to faery ointment in any of your local stories?

When you have a dream or two that feel like fae dreams, take your notes of them to your hawthorn tree and read them aloud, or tell the tree about them. Or sit at your altar, make an offering to the ancestors and your guide, and tell them about your dreams. If you feel puzzled by them you can ask for further clarification. Let yourself gently ponder the imagery in your dreams and see what arises.

What herbs have you read about that might be useful in magical housework, honouring the fae? Look them up and see what other magical or healing properties they have (and take note if they are toxic/poisonous!). Might you be able to grow one or two as potted plants for your altar?

Questions to Ponder

What rules and taboos have you encountered?
Why do you think they might be in place?
What patterns have you noticed around them?
What might you have to offer the spirits that choose to work with you?
What are you willing to offer, and for what benefits?
What do you feel is the connection between dreamland and Faeryland?

Chapter 6

Returning Home

"But Thomas, you must hold your tongue,
Whatever you may hear or see,
For if a word you should chance to speak,
You will never get back to your own country."

He has gotten a coat of the even cloth,
And a pair of shoes of velvet green,
And till seven years were past and gone
True Thomas on earth was never seen.

Your Own Tale

Over the course of our adventure together you have hopefully found some local tales of spirits. If not, now is the time to read a bit of local folklore! Choose the story you've found which best resonates with your feelings about the fae, or which illustrates what you see as a good relationship with the land spirits of your area. It is up to you and your resources on quite how local you get, you may even have tales about your town, or perhaps resources are hard to come by so you've got something which is based in your country, but not quite your area of it. Either is fine as long as you feel it is a story that fits where you are doing this work.

Read the story to yourself and consider the landscape. Does the story describe part of the landscape in which it is set? Does it speak of patterns of weather or seasons? Are there plants or animals that feature in the story that you recognise from your environment? Look for any reflections of the physical world about you in the stories.

Now consider the events of the tale. Are there specific actions that characters take which strike you as important, either as things that should be done, or things that should be avoided? Look for examples of instructions which the faery beings give that the human cannot help but go against, through accident or through nature. Why do you think those instructions were given? Why do you think they were difficult to follow? What do they tell you about human-faery relationships?

Finally, consider what you wish to take away from the story and implement in your work with the faeries? Is there an image that you can include on your altar which you feel will connect you to their magic? Is there a clue in the tale as to where you might find a Faery Gateway (as in Chapter 4), where their energies might be particularly strong in your land? Are there clues about how your local faeries most like to be approached, what offerings they might like, what they might help you with in return?

Take your story outside to a Faery Gateway if you can, or to your altar. Make an offering to them and, dedicating the act to their honour, read the story out loud. Ask, at the end, if they can show you what from that story is good to remember and allow yourself some time to listen to the responses. If you struggle with this, request that you get the information in your dreams tonight and make sure you note down your dreams in the morning!

Being Inspired

I hope you can see from the materials in this book that there is a wealth of information hiding in plain sight for working with the hidden folk! Stories you may already know hold keys to this magic, and to the possibility of building healthy relationships with the spirits.

Perhaps you might like to write your own story, the story of how you found them, or how you hope to. As they are beings of life, they often encourage great creativity, and they are known to have a deep love of creative folks. If you paint, make music, cook, garden, doodle, write… you can make something as a gift for them and then invite them to bless the work you do. The stories are full of inspiration, and I've spent many years trying to capture experiences I've had with the faeries themselves in pictures and words. Allow yourself to be inspired and they will provide you with more muses than you ever thought possible!

Practice 18. Rebuilding Your Altar

Now might be a good time to look over the items on your altar. How has your understanding shifted? How has your relationship begun to evolve? Does your altar still reflect this? Take some time to clean your altar and if it feels appropriate change the items, images or layout to better reflect where you are now. If you've been doing this throughout the chapters then even better!

Look at what the land is doing outside. Are there flowers blooming? Are the trees budding? Is it rainy season? Is there snow? Consider including something on your altar which relates to the land and weather outside. As the seasons change, change this aspect to reflect the land to help you keep an awareness of and a connection to the spirits outside.

You may also wish to include something which represents the being which has been your guide and support through this work, if you haven't already.

Honouring the House Fae

In many stories we find faery spirits who help around the house. In Scotland they are called Brownies, in Norway they are known as Nissa, in Russia there are Kobolds, and in modern tales they've become known as House Elves. The well-known story of the cobbler and the elves, wherein a poor cobbler is helped by elves in the night to make beautiful shoes that earn him enough money to live comfortably, is a good example of these tales. In the end the cobbler sees that the elves have only rags to wear and he makes them beautiful outfits in thanks. On receiving the outfits, they leave forever. Sometimes this is because the cobbler made the clothes so he needn't be ashamed that raggedy elves were making the shoes, and they take offense. Other times it is because they love the clothes so much, they leave in excitement.

I have theories as to why clothing isn't appropriate as an offering, the main one we discussed in Chapter 3 being that it is a way of imposing our view of what is appropriate on beings who are not human, not bound by our conventions, not even, often, human shaped! Regardless, it is clear that there are faery beings who like to help around the house and who like specific offerings.

They are also said to help people who work hard themselves, rewarding dedication and effort in the same way Mother Holla did in the last chapter's story. These are the beings to call upon when you need help clearing negativity from your home, or if you need an extra bit of assistance in getting your home clean and tidy (or keeping it that way!). Ultimately you are living together, part of a team of housemates, and so working together to keep the space nice makes sense.

Where a house is not already home to such a spirit, as can happen, there are also traditions of creating a welcoming space and inviting one to move in. See what your circumstances are and decide what you think might be best. You may be able to ask your guide to mediate for you, or if you have a relationship with a deity, perhaps they will help to ensure you're inviting a kind spirit in. Do not just open the doors and leave out the welcome mat, however, as not all spirits are benevolent, remember? Common sense, as always, applies here too.

Practice 19. Offerings to House Spirits
Traditional offerings for house spirits include;

Certain foods, often milk and honey or pudding.
Fresh, clean water for them to use.

A clean space by the fire/heater for them to rest in
Cleaning the space physically.

Have a look through your stories and see what mention of house spirits you can find, and what gifts or behaviour they have appreciated. You may wish to make a space for them on your altar, or you might feel it is more appropriate (or more practical) to leave them a dish of milk and honey or a glass of water on the kitchen windowsill, by the fireplace, or somewhere else you feel they might visit. Remember to replace it every day, these faeries will definitely object to mouldy milk!

You can pour out the old offerings outside or down the sink, depending on how you feel. I always pour mine outside, returning the physical component to the land it came from, as this little bit of extra effort feels important to me. It may not be practical or relevant for you however, so decide for yourself, and listen to your house spirits, for what you feel is best.

Moving Forwards

In this book you have learned many different aspects of folkloric inspired faery magic, you have built an altar for this work, gathered stories and local lore, and begun to develop your own relationships with faery beings, especially your Faery Guide and the Hounds, who you can continue to call on for protection and guidance in this work. You will also have developed an understanding of appropriate offerings for different places and kinds of beings.

As you continue on this path, if you choose to, make a note of which offerings seem to feel most right in which situations. Notice which get the best responses in terms of signs, messages, dream responses, or feelings. By doing this you get to know what your local faery folk most appreciate.

Continue keeping a dream journal, especially when you notice faery dreams or when you have asked for faery contact that night. The patterns will become clear over time.

Try to practice the "Dropped and Open Attention" from Chapter 3, or a similar practice, at least once a week to increase your ability to move between the states of mind useful for faery contact and everyday modes of being. This is also useful to put yourself in a trance-state for communicating with faery beings such as your guide.

You may find that you encounter other, specific faery beings. As they make themselves known to you treat them as you would any stranger and get to know them slowly. Gradually build up to a friendship or a working partnership, depending on what feels appropriate. Remember to call on your Guide to mediate if you feel unsure.

Have a look back over the tools and material I have shared with you in this book and decide which aspects were most useful for you. Make a note of which ones you would like to integrate into your life and continue using those regularly. Keep a record of your favourite tales and the insights you've gained from them, and know that you may well discover new things about the tales and the beings you encounter over time. Your understanding will change and that is good. This is about living relationships, not dogma. You may well find yourself disagreeing with things that I have said, in fact I hope you do. What I have shared is not gospel, there is no "Faery Bible", and I can only show you what I have learned in my lifetime of working with the fae and their tales. They may well show you different things. That does not make either of us more right than the other, follow your instincts. As you worked through this book you will have supported the development of your intuition and your ability to listen to the Fae, to understand what they are sharing, and to trust your own reactions. Although this journey is never done, I hope that you now feel as though you have a clear idea of how to find the right path for you!

Practice 20. Making a Faery Charm

To carry you forward in this work you may wish to make a charm which can remind you of the presence of the Faery realm in your daily life. A holey stone is a traditional charm, so if you are lucky enough to be wandering somewhere pebbly be open to receiving one from the Fair Folk.

As magical practitioners, however, we can also choose to be proactive and crafting a charm is always a good option. There are many stories of magic bags in folklore, so let us start there.

Take a piece of cloth, preferably in a natural material such as cotton, but it doesn't have to be.

Sew it into a little pouch and add a drawstring long enough to hang it around your neck.

Place it on your altar under the full moon overnight and ask for the blessings of the faeries on it.

Hang it around your neck and either go for a wander with the intention of finding a gift from the faeries to keep in your magic bag, or, using the "Dropped and Open Attention" exercise in Chapter 3, take yourself into a sense of faery and doodle or write words on a piece of paper for five minutes. When you're done look over what you've done, pick out the images, shapes or words which you feel are a gift from them, and transfer that onto a nice piece of card which you can fold up and keep in your bag. (You can do both if you wish.)

From now on, if you can, wear this bag whenever you do faery related work and use it to keep little gifts you find from them.

Sometimes you'll feel that something in your bag has done its work and it can be returned to the earth, and you may find that in time the bag itself needs replacing. This is all fine. Follow the guidance of your intuition and the Fae beings who are working with you.

Practice 21. An Offering for Your Guide

Throughout this work you have been supported by a faery being, your Guide. As we bring this book to a close, now is a good time to check in with them. Choose a gift for them, whether a poem, story, song, picture, favourite food, or something else, it is up to you.

In front of your altar, light a candle and get into a receptive state of mind. Call to your guide. When you feel their presence, offer them the gift you have brought and ask if they need anything from you at this point. Listen to their response (and negotiate if necessary). If you would like to continue working with them, ask if they would continue working with you. If you get the sense that your work together is coming to an end then you can ask if they will introduce you to another guide if you choose. Be open to their answers.

Spend a little time together if you feel it appropriate, listening to and sharing with them how you feel about the journey you have been on and the time you have shared.

When it is time, say farewell and return to your altar. Snuff out the candle and make a note of anything you need or want to remember.

Integration

Take a look over what you've done during this work. Have a look at your altar, spaces you've made for offerings to the house fae, anything you've put together for your ancestors. Think about the places you've visited, your hawthorn tree, faery mounds or wells, or even the liminal space of your doorway. What offerings can you take to those places? What objects have you made or gathered? Which still feel relevant and useful?

Look back over your notes from the past month. What patterns do you notice? Which themes are repeating themselves? What times or places seem most suitable to you for connecting with the faery spirits? Which activities have been your favourites? Which have felt wrong for you? Which ones might you continue after this book is over? How might you integrate things you've learned into your regular life, and magical practice if you have one?

Questions to Ponder

What does "faery" mean to you now?

How might you honour your house spirits and local land spirits in the future?

What impact has having an altar in your space dedicated to this work had on you and your life?

What are the stories that have resonated with you the most?

Where might you look next?

Who could you talk to about your local folklore?

Is there a storytelling circle nearby you could join?

How do you feel about finding magic in stories?

Chapter 7

Integration and Practice

As you've worked through the material contained in this book you will have seen the way I've taken the clues in the folktales and myths within and translated them into practical ways you can build your own practice of working with faery spirits, and I've encouraged you to investigate your own local stories so that you can uncover the threads which apply to your landscape and your cultural background.

Sometimes, however, it can be hard to work out how to apply the clues that we find, and when we do, it can be tempting to treat our choices as dogma. Just as faery spirits, and spirits in general, are not particularly easy to box into tidy categories, so too are our magical practices and our relationships with these beings fluid and prone to shapeshifting. Let us, then, look at what we can do with the clues that we find, and how we can take the interesting pieces of information and integrate them into our practice.

UPG vs Lore

Because this kind of work is built on relationship, it can be very personal, so it is useful to distinguish between the pieces that work for us personally, and the pieces that apply universally. This is where two reconstructionist terms can come in handy.

In certain pagan paths there is an emphasis on reconstructing what a particular historical group were likely to have done. In those practices it is important to have the correct information – or as correct as possible given the evidence available. But there is still an acknowledgment that when one works with spirits, gods, wights, and living, changing magic, those beings we work with may give us new information which we cannot "verify" in the stories or archaeological records. That doesn't mean it isn't useful, it just means we shouldn't claim that it is "reconstructed". Over time, however, enough people may have the experience of that same information, and experience it being useful, that it eventually becomes a *"verified* personal gnosis", verified, in this instance, by the community.

And so it is the same with faeries. We can see in many stories that faeries journey to our world through water, or earthen mounds, and so this is part of "faery lore". My experience is that they can also appear at rock music concerts, enjoying the energy of the dancing, and so my "unverified personal gnosis" is that rock musical events could also operate as temporary gateways between their world and ours. If enough people also experience this then perhaps it will become verified, but that doesn't matter to my practice (and, of course, the Fair Folk are known historically to have a soft spot for human music). For me, I can go to a sacred well or mound, or a rock concert to tap into that magic and commune with spirits. But when I teach, I only recommend the first two, because my UPG may only work for me and my relationship with them. Do feel free to be open to it, though, and see what happens. Just ensure you have a strong enough energetic practice that you can protect yourself from the roiling mass of human energy and emotion at an event like that!

There is a third aspect to this, however; that of interpretation. Regardless of whether it is based on lore or experience, on suggestions someone has given you or an intuitive hunch, all information requires interpretation. Even the stories, laid out in voice or ink, need reading and understanding.

So, whatever you do, wherever you go, remember that this is *your* relationship, your practice, and your understanding. This book contains parts of *mine*, and what you do with it will be between you and the faeries. If and when we choose to share what we've learned, how we've interpreted it, and what we do with that, then being honest and aware of how we've reached that point, as much as we can, is important for allowing other people to reach their own relationship with this magical path.

Finding Clues

The stories that we unearth have always been recorded through a human being who has interpreted the material and expressed part of their understanding, and our cultural background will shape how we, in turn, understand what they are sharing. But when something resonates with us, we remember it and share it. Stories are rewritten and retold in many ways, and the core parts of them are the parts that remain more or less the same with every iteration.One way of finding core truths in a tale, then, is to look at different versions and see which aspects are repeated.

- Which parts matter so much that we cannot let them go?
- Which parts of the story are key turning points? What are central symbols or objects that are important to the tale and the people within it?
- Which behaviours are warned for or against?
- What actions are rewarded, and which are punished?
- What is the outcome of those actions?

Draw a map, whether with words or images, of the pieces of the tale that strike you as important. Look at the overall pattern too. If you see something which feels like a later addition, perhaps a moral imperative tacked on the end, see if it is an interpretation of the person who was sharing or recording the tale of something underneath it. For example, in the myth of Blodeuwedd we meet a lady made of flowers who is portrayed as betraying her husband. But calling the activity a betrayal presents it with a moral front that obscures the piece that she was making a *choice* for herself. The wild magic of the land could not be forced into granting sovereignty to the husband chosen for her, and forcing that feral fae spirit into a role unconsenting led to great pain for all involved. Looking underneath the activity depicted reveals something about the magic of the land and a way of treating it which is not recommended... So, consider; what is that piece you've found hiding?

Turning Clues into Practice

Once you have gathered your puzzle pieces, you now have the opportunity to integrate them into your magical practice. Let us take the tale of *Thomas the Rhymer* again, who has guided us through this book. In his ballad we learn about the nature of the Queen of Elfhame, the gateway of hawthorn and the journey to the otherworld across water and blood. And we learn what happens when he carefully follows the instructions he was given.

In the end, Thomas is given "shoes of green", and so he is clothed in the colour of faery magic. His very foundation, where his body touches the earth, is held in their gift. Thomas has, by journeying to the otherworld, eating the food offered, and working diligently as the beloved of the Queen, become part of that world. He can move between there and here, and it is said that he did not ultimately die but rather returned to his Queen's side, which suggests that he has the ability to choose when he journeys in each direction.

Thomas, then, has been recognised as a human who understands Faeryland, and who has become partly transformed by his connection with them. This suggests that he is a good being to contact for guidance in making the trip between the realms yourself.

Perhaps your practice involves journeying meditations, in which case you might take the knowledge of Thomas as guide into your work by calling on his help when you begin your journeys to Faeryland. Perhaps, instead, your practice involves communicating with faery spirits, and he might become someone you request assistance in bridging the worlds for them to draw closer to here, or translating the communications to help with ease of understanding.

Or perhaps you might, once you have built a strong relationship with True Thomas and the faery folk, request his blessing on an item of green to wear yourself, to keep their connection with you and assist you in making the journey there and back again whenever you wear it.

In your local stories, perhaps you find that the faery folk most often turn up in taverns, and tend to ask for a specific drink or meal. This might inform the offerings that you make to earn their favour.

Or perhaps you take on one of the taboos that they give to the human that is walking with them, one that resonates, like a period of silence, or a vow of honesty like Thomas' tongue that cannot lie.

Allow these things to grow and develop over time. As you spend more time working with them you will find that they guide you to the information and stories which are most useful for your relationship, and you'll begin to develop or deepen your sense of which of the options before you is the bonny, bonny path to fair Elfland…

Ethics and Living

One of the features you may notice in these stories is how much of everyday life there is in them. Strange things happen alongside the most normal activities. Magical beings engage in mundane tasks. The faery ring is found on the way home from a perfectly unremarkable evening. And the major rites of passage and aspects of life that feature are as integral to human life now as they ever were; birth, puberty, marriage, love, sex, illness, work, poverty, luck, death, and adventure.

These stories are not an escape from life, they are windows onto ways we can live. Mirrors held up to values and relationships.

The distance between where you sit and the land of Elfhame is merely a blink. The spirit realm can be found in dreams and wishes, in the moments of dozing and hope, and in the space between one room and another. It is not some far off land, but is, rather, right here. And so we find ourselves looking at the pieces of the puzzle and pondering, how does this fit into my life today?

Some of us will spend hours, days, weeks, months, and years, honing specific techniques and skills to do complex, intense, magical work. But for most of us, we can, and must, find the magical alongside the mundane. In this book we've looked at the process of making offerings, of keeping an altar, of dreaming with the spirits and of honouring the ancestors and the spirits of our homes. These pieces of everyday magic remind us that the only real veil between our world and theirs is that of our forgetfulness.

We can also find important ethical directives within our tales of them which can inform our way of living in the world. Some aspects which I find highlighted are:

Honesty and integrity
Respect for all beings
Maintaining appropriate boundaries
Hospitality
Reciprocity
Avoiding entitlement

As I see these, they all come down to striving to be in healthy partnership with all the beings of the world, starting with ourselves and the spirits of the land and magic nearby whose home feeds and supports us. You, however, may find something different in the tales, because each relationship is just that, a unique, living, relationship.

Questions to Ponder
What place does UPG have in your practice?

How might you integrate folklore (and magical lore) into your practice in the modern world?

What guidance for living might you take from the stories you have gathered?

What is your ethical stance on things such as honesty, self-sacrifice, helping strangers, caring for the land?

What is ethically important to you?

What have you taken from the work in this book?

How have you built and deepened your relationship with the spirit world?

What are the different types of spirits and faeries that you've encountered?

How might you support others in navigating this path with the knowledge to do so safely?

What will you take forward?

What is your next step?

And how can you honour the beings who you have met during this work now?

Epilogue

Happy Journeying

And so we reach the end of our journey together. I hope you've enjoyed the path we have shared so far and are looking forward to where it might lead you next.

It is quite likely that you will find, or perhaps already have found, material which directly contradicts that which I have shared here, how you reconcile that with your practice is entirely up to you, but my recommendation is always to have an open mind and explore. How does that which you find match up with that which you know? Where does the information have its roots? Does it match your experiences, or might it give you a new light to understand your earlier experiences with? If it doesn't fit, then consider why. The folklore, stories, and experiences of those that have walked this path before can help us to navigate our own journey. But we do well to remember that not all information is correct, not all conflicting information is false, and not all true information is useful. In your relationship to the spirits, the truth is between you and them. I know, without a doubt, that the fae are real beings, as real as you and I, and with discernment, respect, and care, we can build partnerships and friendships which honour all involved. Apply those principles to all you come across, including what I have shared, and you'll find your own way, as each of us must.

Remember that you can, and should, ask the faeries and your guide for their input too. If you find a piece of information, mull it over, examine it, and sit with it in a trance state, listening to the responses of the fair folk that you work with. Which way are they guiding you? And which of the many spirits that you could be encountering are sat with you today?

Until next time... I wish you all the best on your next adventure.

In delight,
Halo x

Beltane-tide 2021
With dolphins and magic on the horizon.

About Halo

Halo is a practising witch and a lifelong lover of magic. She is a devotee of Freya and the Faery Queen, a lover of the Welsh gods, a storyteller, philosopher, and sensual witch working to (re)enchant the world.

Led deep into the wilds of Wales by dreams and wandering words, Halo's magic has always focused on listening to the spirits of the land, an animistic path which introduced her to the Welsh deities, with an embodied approach to their craft and a strong interest in the connections between spirit and human communities, stories and experience, and magic and everyday life.

Halo is trained in Reclaiming Witchcraft, an initiated witch, a member the Order of Bards Ovates and Druids, the creator of The Enchanted Academy(TEA), and co-founder of The Star Club.

A Note to You, Dear Reader

Dear reader,

I am so happy you decided to join me on this journey, and I really hope you've enjoyed your time with me and these spirits. If you haven't already, you are very welcome to join the small, but growing, community at The Enchanted Academy (TEA), where there is space for students and enthusiasts of faery magic to chat, share experiences, ask questions, support each other, and keep in touch on the journey ahead.

If you've enjoyed this journey then I'd love for you to leave me a review on your favourite book-sites, even a few words (or just the stars) really do help others to find what they're looking for!

And finally... Thank you. Just, thank you. For your support in buying this book, for placing your trust in my work, and for honouring the magic and spirits by giving your time and energy to engaging with the process in whatever way you have. I hope this continues to inspire and support you in building these relationships and your own magical practice for many years to come.

You can find me and The Enchanted Academy at www. theenchantedacademy.com and on my website; www.haloquin. net

Further Reading

General Faery Magic

RJ Stewart, *Living World of Faery*, (Mercury Publishing, 1999) – this was my first proper look at faery magic beyond the new age model, and RJ Stewart's work remains one of my favourite sources of inspiration for engagement, even with the more ceremonial influences creeping in later.

Brian Froud and Jessica Macbeth, *Faery Oracle*, Book/cards (Atria Books, 2001) – not strictly folkloric, but drawing inspiration from those sources and from interactions with the wild faery magic.

Halo Quin, *Pagan Portals: Your Faery Magic* (Moon Books, 2015) is my introduction to tapping into the magic we talk about in this book within yourself, with more of a focus on personal practice rooted in modern techniques.

Collections of Fairy and Folk Stories

Note: not all Fairy tales are about faeries, but even when they aren't most of them give clues for interacting with the otherworld or magical situations, beings and objects. There is a debate within academia about what makes something a fairy tale, with many academics opting to call these kinds of stories "wonder tales" instead. For our purposes, however, folk tales, fairy tales and even myths and legends often contain clues to faery work!

The Ballad of Thomas the Rhymer is from the Borders of Scotland and is known as one of the *Child Ballads* because it was collected by Francis James Child in the 1800s. You can read the *Child Ballads* here: *www.traditionalmusic.co.uk/child-ballads*

The tale of Pwyll's Descent in Chapter 2 comes from *Y Mabinogi*, a collection of Welsh legends recorded in the 13th Century. The first English translation was by Lady Charlotte Guest. You can find retellings of all four branches of Y Mabinogi in my previous book, *Pagan Portals; Gods and Goddesses of Wales* (Moon Books, 2019).

The website Sacred Texts has a huge amount of Fairy tales, from many cultures: *www.sacred-texts.com*

Andrew Lang's Fairy Books, which are each named for the colour of their cover, are classic collections written (or rewritten) for children, and are still in print in several versions. They do tend towards the literary rather than the folkloric, however, so be wary of taking them at face value.

The Grimms' Fairy Tales is a major classic anthology, collected in Germany by the two brothers, Jakob and Wilhelm Grimm. While you can read them online, there is now a beautiful collection of these tales by a Grimm scholar who has translated them back as close to the original stories that the Grimms recorded as possible. After the brothers first published them, they came under pressure to edit them for the children of the time, so some of the rougher aspects got polished out. If you can, then, I recommend *The Original Folk and Fairy Tales of the Brothers Grimm*, translated and edited by Jack Zipes. If not, again, Sacred Texts is a wonderful resource.

In Britain there are marvellous collections of folklore based in each county, published by The History Press, including *Ceredigion Folk Tales* by Peter Stevenson, and others in that range, or covering a broader area such as *Dancing with Trees – Eco-Tales from the British Isles* by Allison Galbraith and Alette J Willis.

Fairy-Human Relations

You can explore more about how people have worked with the Fair Folk historically in books such as *Cunning Folk and Familiar Spirits*, By Emma Wilby.

Interactions with the Faery Queen/s specifically has been written about in *The Faerie Queens*, an anthology by Avalonia Press.

Wights and Ancestors – Heathenry in a Living Landscape, by

Jenny Blain explores methods for engaging with your local landwights.

Elves, Wights and Trolls by K. Gundarsson discusses human-faery interactions within a Germanic/Norse/Heathen context.

Older, classic texts include *The Fairy Faith in Celtic Countries* by Evans-Wentz, and *The Secret Commonwealth* by Robert Kirk.

Charms, Prayers, Spells and Herbs

Carmina Gadelica, Volume 1, by Alexander Carmicheal, [1900], at sacred-texts.com – this is a useful resource for traditional Scottish prayers and folk charms which can be used, adapted and allowed to inspire you in your practices.

Charms, Spells and Formulas, by Ray Marlbrough – written based in the American tradition of Conjure, this small book contains a lot of suggestions for specific herbs, oils and washes you can make for various uses, including cleansing and home blessing. If you are working in a place with a strong history of conjure, or if you have a connection to it, this might be useful for you.

Encyclopaedia of Magical Herbs, by Scott Cunningham – a resource for discovering which herbs are good for which magic, recommended to me by professional magical herbalists.

Physicians of Myddfai, Translated and edited by Terry Breverton – the titular Physicians lived in the 13th Century in Wales and were renowned for their healing skills. The story goes that they learned it from their faery mother, the Lady of the Lake, Llyn-y-Fan Fach, and that tale is collected in this book, alongside many of the cures they documented. Their legacy still lives and you can even visit their home village of Myddfai, and the lake itself. Common sense is advised if utilising their cures, of course, as with everything.

Other Magical Practices

Michael Harner, *The Way of the Shaman,* (HarperSanFrancisco, 1992). Harner was an anthropologist who studied various magical practices described in anthropological texts as traditional shamanism and developed the techniques he learned into "core shamanism", which has strongly influenced a lot of practical magic in modern paganism. The techniques he describes can be helpful for developing a direct relationship with spirits and journeying between worlds.

Jenny Blain, *Nine Worlds of Seid-Magic*, looks at the evidence we have for magical practices in Northern Europe and shows how they might be understood and integrated into a spirit-based practice today.

JRR Tolkien, *On Fairy-Stories* – while not strictly an explicit magical practice, Tolkien's essay on Faerie is an excellent contemplation on the nature of enchantment and the role of the otherworldly in our life. Besides, world weaving and bespelling through language is, after all, an act of enchantment.

~ a note on links ~

The internet being a fickle thing, links are subject to changing, where a paper book is much slower to change. To offset this, I've created a page on my website which I'll endeavour to keep updated (and expanding) at www.TheEnchantedAcademy.com

The Ballad of True Thomas

TRUE THOMAS lay on grassy bank,
And he beheld a lady gay,
A lady that was brisk and bold,
Come riding over the fernie brae.

Her skirt was of the grass-green silk,
Her mantel of the velvet fine,
And on every lock of her horse's mane
Hung fifty silver bells and nine.

True Thomas he took off his hat,
And bowed down to his knee:
"All hail, mighty Queen of Heaven!
For your peer on earth I never did see."

"O no, O no, True Thomas," she says,
"That name does not belong to me;
I am but the queen of fair Elfland,
And I've come here to visit thee."

"But you must go with me now, Thomas,
True Thomas, you must go with me,
For you must serve me seven years,
Through well or woe as may chance to be."

She turned about her milk-white steed,
And took True Thomas up behind,
And aye whene'er her bridle rang,
The steed flew swifter than the wind.

For forty days and forty nights
He wade through red blood to the knee,
And he saw neither sun nor moon,
But heard the roaring of the sea.

O they rode on, and further on,
Until they came to a garden green:
"Light down, light down, ye lady free,
Some of that fruit let me pull to thee."

"O no, O no, True Thomas," she says,
"That fruit must not be touched by thee,
For all the plagues that are in hell
Light on the fruit of this country."

"But I have a loaf here in my lap,
Likewise a bottle of claret wine,
And now 'ere we go farther on,
We'll rest a while, and ye may dine."

When he had eaten and drunk his fill,
"Lay down your head upon my knee,"
The lady said, "'ere we climb yon hill,
And I will show you fair things three."

"O see you not that narrow road,
So thick beset with thorns and briars?
That is the path of righteousness,
Though after it but few enquire."

"And see not you that broad broad road,
That lies across yon lillie leven?
That is the path of wickedness,
Though some call it the road to heaven."

"And see not you that bonny road,
Which winds about the fernie brae?
That is the road to fair Elfland,
Where you and I this night will go."

"But Thomas, you must hold your tongue,
Whatever you may hear or see,
For if a word you should chance to speak,
You will never get back to your own country."

He has gotten a coat of the even cloth,
And a pair of shoes of velvet green,
And till seven years were past and gone
True Thomas on earth was never seen.

~ Note, this version has been Anglicised for ease of reading for those unfamiliar with old Scots dialects.

You may also like

Pagan Portals - Your Faery Magic
Discover what it means to be fey and unlock your natural power

978-1-78535-076-4 (Paperback)
978-1-78535-077-1 (ebook)

MOON
BOOKS

PAGANISM & SHAMANISM

What is Paganism? A religion, a spirituality, an alternative belief system, nature worship? You can find support for all these definitions (and many more) in dictionaries, encyclopaedias, and text books of religion, but subscribe to any one and the truth will evade you. Above all Paganism is a creative pursuit, an encounter with reality, an exploration of meaning and an expression of the soul. Druids, Heathens, Wiccans and others, all contribute their insights and literary riches to the Pagan tradition. Moon Books invites you to begin or to deepen your own encounter, right here, right now.

If you have enjoyed this book, why not tell other readers by posting a review on your preferred book site.

Recent bestsellers from Moon Books are:

Journey to the Dark Goddess
How to Return to Your Soul
Jane Meredith
Discover the powerful secrets of the Dark Goddess and
transform your depression, grief and pain into healing
and integration.
Paperback: 978-1-84694-677-6 ebook: 978-1-78099-223-5

Shamanic Reiki
Expanded Ways of Working with Universal Life Force Energy
Llyn Roberts, Robert Levy
Shamanism and Reiki are each powerful ways of healing; together,
their power multiplies. *Shamanic Reiki* introduces techniques to
help healers and Reiki practitioners tap ancient healing wisdom.
Paperback: 978-1-84694-037-8 ebook: 978-1-84694-650-9

Pagan Portals – The Awen Alone
Walking the Path of the Solitary Druid
Joanna van der Hoeven
An introductory guide for the solitary Druid, *The Awen Alone* will
accompany you as you explore, and seek out your own place
within the natural world.
Paperback: 978-1-78279-547-6 ebook: 978-1-78279-546-9

A Kitchen Witch's World of Magical Herbs & Plants
Rachel Patterson
A journey into the magical world of herbs and plants, filled with
magical uses, folklore, history and practical magic. By popular
writer, blogger and kitchen witch, Tansy Firedragon.
Paperback: 978-1-78279-621-3 ebook: 978-1-78279-620-6

Medicine for the Soul
The Complete Book of Shamanic Healing
Ross Heaven
All you will ever need to know about shamanic healing and how to
become your own shaman...
Paperback: 978-1-78099-419-2 ebook: 978-1-78099-420-8

Shaman Pathways – The Druid Shaman
Exploring the Celtic Otherworld
Danu Forest
A practical guide to Celtic shamanism with exercises and
techniques as well as traditional lore for exploring the Celtic
Otherworld.
Paperback: 978-1-78099-615-8 ebook: 978-1-78099-616-5

Traditional Witchcraft for the Woods and Forests
A Witch's Guide to the Woodland with Guided Meditations and
Pathworking
Mélusine Draco
A Witch's guide to walking alone in the woods, with guided
meditations and pathworking.
Paperback: 978-1-84694-803-9 ebook: 978-1-84694-804-6

Wild Earth, Wild Soul
A Manual for an Ecstatic Culture
Bill Pfeiffer
Imagine a nature-based culture so alive and so connected,
spreading like wildfire. This book is the first flame...
Paperback: 978-1-78099-187-0 ebook: 978-1-78099-188-7

Naming the Goddess
Trevor Greenfield
Naming the Goddess is written by over eighty adherents and
scholars of Goddess and Goddess Spirituality.
Paperback: 978-1-78279-476-9 ebook: 978-1-78279-475-2

Shapeshifting into Higher Consciousness
Heal and Transform Yourself and Our World with Ancient
Shamanic and Modern Methods
Llyn Roberts
Ancient and modern methods that you can use every day to
transform yourself and make a positive difference in the world.
Paperback: 978-1-84694-843-5 ebook: 978-1-84694-844-2

Readers of ebooks can buy or view any of these bestsellers by
clicking on the live link in the title. Most titles are published in
paperback and as an ebook. Paperbacks are available in traditional
bookshops. Both print and ebook formats are available online.

Find more titles and sign up to our readers' newsletter at
http://www.johnhuntpublishing.com/paganism
Follow us on Facebook at https://www.facebook.com/MoonBooks
and Twitter at https://twitter.com/MoonBooksJHP